THE BRUMBACK LIBRARY

OF VAN WERT COUNTY

VAN WERT, OHIO

GAYLORD

HELEN STEINER RICE
Ambassador of Sunshine

HELEN STEINER RICE
Ambassador of Sunshine

Ronald Pollitt
and
Virginia Wiltse

Fleming H. Revell
A Division of Baker Book House Co
Grand Rapids, Michigan 49516

Published by Fleming H. Revell
a division of Baker Book House Company
P.O. Box 6287, Grand Rapids, MI 49516-6287

Printed in the United States of America

Library of Congress Cataloging-in-Publication Data

Pollitt, Ronald.
    Helen Steiner Rice: ambassador of sunshine / Ronald Pollitt and Virginia Wiltse.
       p.   cm.
   ISBN 0-8007-1701-5
   1. Rice, Helen Steiner—Biography. 2. Women poets, American—20th century—Biography. 3. Christian biography—United States. I. Wiltse, Virginia. II. Title.
PS3568.I28Z83 1994
811'.54—dc20
[B]   93-36520

CONTENTS

She looks out at you, precociously, from pictures taken nearly a hundred years ago—little Helen Steiner, only two or three years of age—with her big brown eyes, honey-colored curls, ready smile, and poise that seems vaguely disturbing in one so young. Even then, just after the turn of the century, there was something exceptional about this child who called herself "Honey Tiner" when she was barely old enough to talk. She was certainly gifted; God seemed to smile on her from the first moment she appeared on the planet, and, although she had no way of knowing it in those early years, Helen Steiner Rice was also one of those rare creatures destined to succeed, as if by magic, in everything they attempted throughout their lives.

As time passed, those childhood traits of self-assurance, intelligence, resolution, and optimism—the ones that marked young Miss Steiner as an extraordinary woman—only grew stronger. Helen's story—how she left an idyllic childhood in a port town on Lake Erie, traveled across the country as a lecturer, overcame personal tragedy, triumphed through determination and talent, and eventually achieved international recognition as an inspirational poet—is a singular realization of the American dream. A product of her time but ahead of it, as grounded in practical realities as she was at home with eternal truths, Helen Steiner Rice was and remains a uniquely

ACKNOWLEDGMENTS

The authors are especially grateful to Pamela Pollitt, C.P.A., and David Wiltse, M.D., for their patience and cooperation during the preparation of this book.

We also appreciate the assistance of Mrs. Virginia J. Ruehlmann, administrator of the Helen Steiner Rice Foundation, for without her help and encouragement Mrs. Rice's achievements would never have received the attention they merit.

Many others also deserve thanks. Among them are the trustees of the Helen Steiner Rice Foundation—Willis Gradison, Jr., Eugene Ruehlmann, Esq., Benjamin Sottile, and Donald Weston —whose support contributed significantly to the completion of the project. Gertrude Steiner's cooperation was equally as important, for she provided the authors with invaluable information prior to her death in March 1992. In addition, we acknowledge the assistance given in the course of our research by Albert C. Doane of the Black River Historical Society, Lorain, Ohio; Joe Jeffries, Research Librarian, Lorain Public Library; Joe M. Herbst of the Zion Memorial Church, Moraine, Ohio; and Nancy Horlacher and Sue Steinke, Research Librarians, Dayton and Montgomery County Public Library. Our portrait of Mrs. Rice was made richer and more complete due to the generosity of several individuals who shared personal or family letter collections, memorabilia, and recollections with us. In this regard, we thank the Reverend Ernest Bein, Lambert Fitzgerald, Joan Gradison Coe, Willis Gradison, Jr., May Hockley, Robert Reis, and Jack and Loretta Wiedemer. We are also grateful to Aztec Video Productions of Cincinnati for assistance in restoring and reproducing many decades-old photographs. To the dozens of others who have shared with us their memories of Helen Steiner Rice, we extend our most sincere appreciation.

8

Helen
Steiner Rice
Ambassador
of Sunshine

The
Heart
Remembers
Vividly

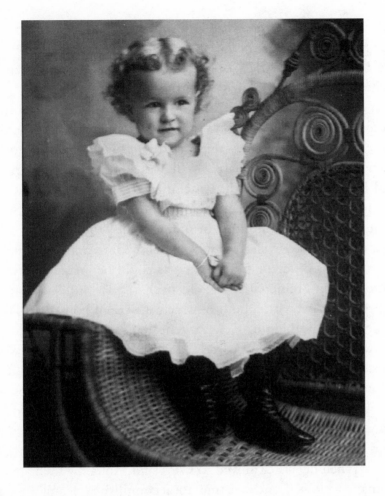

At the early age of three, Helen already exhibited remarkable poise and self-assurance.

American phenomenon. She was a child of the country's heartland, an Ohioan born in Lorain who died in Cincinnati.

Lorain, Ohio, spreads across the southern shores of Lake Erie at the mouth of the Black River, thirty miles west of Cleveland. At the turn of the twentieth century, Lorain's heart beat to the tempo of commerce and industry that made northern Ohio the industrial core of an America ready to assume world leadership. Although Lorain was young—incorporated as a municipality only four years

The Heart Remembers Vividly

earlier—it was nevertheless an area of steady economic growth and power. Lorain was a vibrant city in 1900, one that had grown up on the "heavy industries" of iron, steel, coal, and shipping, and all of its residents felt confident about the future.

If someone bisected the state of Ohio from north to south on an axis starting in Lorain and ending in Cincinnati, he would be struck by the remarkable contrasts that characterized one of the anchor states of the Midwest. Lorain was new, industrial, maritime, and bursting with growth. Cincinnati, on the other hand, had been growing since the eighteenth century, and by 1900 its residents felt a certain amount of pride in the "Queen City of the Midwest." It was, in short, a well-established metropolis with deep roots, one as different from Lorain as could be imagined. Yet the life of Helen Steiner Rice moved back and forth upon that axis between the two cities, both of which she called home.

Certainly, nothing in Helen's genealogical roots indicated that she would grow up to become a trailblazer whose writings would affect thousands of lives. Her parents—Anna Bieri and John Steiner—were humble people, both born in 1872 on farms near Wooster, Ohio. The Bieris were immigrants from Switzerland who struggled to survive the daily hardships of agricultural life. Anna Bieri longed to escape the farm and its barely settled rural environment. When her sister moved to Cleveland, Anna, by then a young woman, followed and became an accomplished seamstress and dress designer. Her cleverness with a sewing machine soon won a large and influential following. Experience taught Anna Bieri that if a woman could find a path to success, she should take it.

The Steiner family, by contrast, had emigrated from what is now Germany, and were more fortunate than the Bieris. Dairy farmers, they found the land northeast of Wooster on the Chippewa River, near Sterling, Ohio, perfectly suited for practicing the skills they had brought from Europe. In time, the Steiners even branched out and acquired a popular restaurant on the busy rail line running

Anna Bieri Steiner, Helen's mother, was an accomplished seamstress in Cleveland before her marriage and move to Lorain, Ohio.

through Sterling. While the Bieri family struggled, the Steiners prospered, so it is not surprising that when Anna Bieri met John Steiner and they fell in love, she insisted they seek their fortune off the farm.

Probably tired of rising before dawn every day to milk cows and then work in the family restaurant and definitely eager to please Anna, a dark-haired and dark-eyed beauty, John Steiner proposed that they marry and move north. They were, after all, young and optimistic, and several of John's acquaintances at the restaurant suggested that he could easily find work on the railroad there, where trains moved coal, iron, steel, and other products all hours of the day. He was hired by the Baltimore and Ohio Railway in no

The
Heart
Remembers
Vividly

*John Steiner
(left), Helen's
father, worked
for the railroad
prior to his
untimely
death in the
1918 flu
epidemic.*

Helen
Steiner Rice
*Ambassador
of Sunshine*

time at all, first as a fireman, but was soon promoted to locomotive engineer.

Feeling secure with a bright future stretching before them, John and Anna Steiner married and settled in a modest frame house on Lexington Avenue in Lorain. Their dreams of starting a family came true when, on May 19, 1900, their first child was born. They christened her Helen Elaine, and entered her name on the "cradle roll" of the Twentieth Street Methodist Church near their home. A second daughter, Gertrude, arrived two years later.

John Steiner was a gentle, jovial man who loved fishing, appreciated a good story, enjoyed his work, and provided lovingly for his family. Even as a youth, he believed in the importance of serv-

ACKNOWLEDGMENTS

The authors are especially grateful to Pamela Pollitt, C.P.A., and David Wiltse, M.D., for their patience and cooperation during the preparation of this book.

We also appreciate the assistance of Mrs. Virginia J. Ruehlmann, administrator of the Helen Steiner Rice Foundation, for without her help and encouragement Mrs. Rice's achievements would never have received the attention they merit.

Many others also deserve thanks. Among them are the trustees of the Helen Steiner Rice Foundation—Willis Gradison, Jr., Eugene Ruehlmann, Esq., Benjamin Sottile, and Donald Weston —whose support contributed significantly to the completion of the project. Gertrude Steiner's cooperation was equally as important, for she provided the authors with invaluable information prior to her death in March 1992. In addition, we acknowledge the assistance given in the course of our research by Albert C. Doane of the Black River Historical Society, Lorain, Ohio; Joe Jeffries, Research Librarian, Lorain Public Library; Joe M. Herbst of the Zion Memorial Church, Moraine, Ohio; and Nancy Horlacher and Sue Steinke, Research Librarians, Dayton and Montgomery County Public Library. Our portrait of Mrs. Rice was made richer and more complete due to the generosity of several individuals who shared personal or family letter collections, memorabilia, and recollections with us. In this regard, we thank the Reverend Ernest Bein, Lambert Fitzgerald, Joan Gradison Coe, Willis Gradison, Jr., May Hockley, Robert Reis, and Jack and Loretta Wiedemer. We are also grateful to Aztec Video Productions of Cincinnati for assistance in restoring and reproducing many decades-old photographs. To the dozens of others who have shared with us their memories of Helen Steiner Rice, we extend our most sincere appreciation.

8

Helen
Steiner Rice
Ambassador
of Sunshine

1

The
Heart
Remembers
Vividly

She looks out at you, precociously, from pictures taken nearly a hundred years ago—little Helen Steiner, only two or three years of age—with her big brown eyes, honey-colored curls, ready smile, and poise that seems vaguely disturbing in one so young. Even then, just after the turn of the century, there was something exceptional about this child who called herself "Honey Tiner" when she was barely old enough to talk. She was certainly gifted; God seemed to smile on her from the first moment she appeared on the planet, and, although she had no way of knowing it in those early years, Helen Steiner Rice was also one of those rare creatures destined to succeed, as if by magic, in everything they attempted throughout their lives.

As time passed, those childhood traits of self-assurance, intelligence, resolution, and optimism—the ones that marked young Miss Steiner as an extraordinary woman—only grew stronger. Helen's story—how she left an idyllic childhood in a port town on Lake Erie, traveled across the country as a lecturer, overcame personal tragedy, triumphed through determination and talent, and eventually achieved international recognition as an inspirational poet—is a singular realization of the American dream. A product of her time but ahead of it, as grounded in practical realities as she was at home with eternal truths, Helen Steiner Rice was and remains a uniquely earlier—it was nevertheless an area of steady economic growth and power. Lorain was a vibrant city in 1900, one that had grown up on the "heavy industries" of iron, steel, coal, and shipping, and all of its residents felt confident about the future.

If someone bisected the state of Ohio from north to south on an axis starting in Lorain and ending in Cincinnati, he would be struck by the remarkable contrasts that characterized one of the anchor states of the Midwest. Lorain was new, industrial, maritime, and bursting with growth. Cincinnati, on the other hand, had been growing since the eighteenth century, and by 1900 its residents felt a certain amount of pride in the "Queen City of the Midwest." It was, in short, a well-established metropolis with deep roots, one as different from Lorain as could be imagined. Yet the life of Helen Steiner Rice moved back and forth upon that axis between the two cities, both of which she called home.

Certainly, nothing in Helen's genealogical roots indicated that she would grow up to become a trailblazer whose writings would affect thousands of lives. Her parents—Anna Bieri and John Steiner—were humble people, both born in 1872 on farms near Wooster, Ohio. The Bieris were immigrants from Switzerland who struggled to survive the daily hardships of agricultural life. Anna Bieri longed to escape the farm and its barely settled rural environment. When her sister moved to Cleveland, Anna, by then a young woman, followed and became an accomplished seamstress and dress designer. Her cleverness with a sewing machine soon won a large and influential following. Experience taught Anna Bieri that if a woman could find a path to success, she should take it.

The Steiner family, by contrast, had emigrated from what is now Germany, and were more fortunate than the Bieris. Dairy farmers, they found the land northeast of Wooster on the Chippewa River, near Sterling, Ohio, perfectly suited for practicing the skills they had brought from Europe. In time, the Steiners even branched out and acquired a popular restaurant on the busy rail line running

At the early age of three, Helen already exhibited remarkable poise and self-assurance.

American phenomenon. She was a child of the country's heartland, an Ohioan born in Lorain who died in Cincinnati.

Lorain, Ohio, spreads across the southern shores of Lake Erie at the mouth of the Black River, thirty miles west of Cleveland. At the turn of the twentieth century, Lorain's heart beat to the tempo of commerce and industry that made northern Ohio the industrial core of an America ready to assume world leadership. Although Lorain was young—incorporated as a municipality only four years

The Heart Remembers Vividly

ing others, of having goals greater than self-interest. He passed that devotion to service, as well as a commitment to duty, on to his daughters.

Anna Steiner kept an immaculate house, and for a while retained as clients some of the women for whom she had made clothing in Cleveland. She taught her daughters important lessons about womanhood. They were instructed in how to manage a household, but they also learned about Anna's resourcefulness, skill, and, perhaps most significantly, her ability to fend for herself if the need arose. She instilled in them the belief that women could love and respect men but need not be totally dependent on them. It was a lesson neither girl forgot. Anna also paid special

"Honey Tiner," as Helen called herself, was a charmer even as a toddler.

The Heart Remembers Vividly

16 *As children, Gertrude (left) and Helen (right) often wore clothing made by their mother.*

attention to the spiritual development of her children. A deeply religious person, she did her best to ground them in the fundamentals of Christian living.

Young Helen Steiner also had a role model, equally as influential as her mother, in her Grandma Bieri. Among Helen's favorite childhood memories were those of her grandmother's house, and the dried flowers arranged and preserved in her parlor. Later in life, Helen wrote nostalgically to a friend:

Helen
Steiner Rice
*Ambassador
of Sunshine*

> *The sweet old-fashioned "Easter Flowers"*
> *Reminded me of childhood hours*
> *Spent with my Grandma on the farm*

That held for me such magic charm. . . .
And in my Grandma's "parlor room,"
Reserved for only "COMPANY"
And not for little tykes like me . . .
There stood a table in the center,
And anyone who chanced to enter
Beheld a "dome of crystal glass"
And underneath was a "bouquet"
That I remember to this day. . . .

Far beyond the magic memories of her grandma's home, Helen benefited from the wisdom imparted by Grandma Bieri when she stayed at the Steiner house. After her husband died and her family had grown and moved away from the homestead, Mrs. Bieri was left with the difficult choice of eking out a living on the farm or spending her declining years with her children. She chose the latter, moving regularly from house to house after selling the Bieri property near Wooster. Although it was a hard choice for Elizabeth Bieri, everyone ultimately profited, for the matriarch brought a richness to the lives of her children and grandchildren that stretched far beyond anything she could ever have accomplished if she had stayed on the farm. One of the greatest beneficiaries of her wisdom was the youthful Helen Steiner, who eagerly looked forward to visits Grandma Bieri paid to the Steiner household in Lorain.

Helen's love of the Scriptures, a love she retained throughout her life, was nurtured on her grandmother's lap. The old lady also told the little girl many memorable stories, but one of the most important ones that helped them pass the hours together was that of a tailor who was once visited by Christ. It was a legend Helen would ultimately make famous as the story of the Christmas Guest.

Grandma Bieri may have looked stern and forbidding, but she was a gentle refuge and source of wisdom for young Helen.

Helen
Steiner Rice
*Ambassador
of Sunshine*

Even though her photograph makes Mrs. Bieri appear as an unforgiving taskmaster, she was actually a kindly, understanding woman. In fact, it was because of her gentleness that Grandma Bieri had such a profound impact on Helen and Gertrude Steiner when they were growing up; she never demanded more than they could give, and they were always grateful for her compassion. Although Mrs. Bieri was never comfortable with any language except German, she knew enough English to teach her grand-daughters the basic Christian truths that had sustained her through all the trials of her life. Sometimes, in her broken English, Grandma Bieri would urge little Helen to "spread the Great

Story." Then Helen would assemble her family on the porch or in the yard, climb on a chair, and deliver biblical homilies that astonished everyone. Mrs. Bieri, however, was less surprised than most, muttering in German: "Wie dieses kann prediken!" ["How she can preach!"]

When her grandmother died, Helen felt a great loss, one made harder because Grandma Bieri passed away suddenly. She suffered a heart attack during one of her visits to the Steiner home.

Given Helen's early training, it is not surprising that she was devout. Her love of the Scriptures soon led Helen to win the privilege of teaching Sunday school lessons to children who were barely younger than herself. As she got older, she joined the choir and even directed plays involving youthful members of the congregation. Mildred Faris James was among the childhood friends who tried to coax Helen into joining them for play and roller skating, but Helen, she remembered, "always wanted to be the preacher."

School played nearly as large a role as her church, and during Helen's growing-up years, she stood out as an exceptional student. She attended Lorain's Garden Avenue School, and later, after her family moved to Reid Avenue, the Garfield School. She always scored well, consistently receiving A's in nearly everything except drawing. She loved to read, write, and spend her time with adults in conversation. At the age of ten, Helen Steiner was one of the outstanding students at Garfield School, a child who, by her own admission, "was anxious to become an adult."

But there was another side to Helen, one perhaps best revealed in a picture of Helen and Gertrude together, both wearing white dresses and white stockings, with bows perched precariously in their hair. They look like twin versions of Shirley Temple singing "The Good Ship Lollipop." The photo captures a fundamental truth about Helen, who appears as comfortable in her pose as Gertie seems shy. Helen had already learned how to use the camera to her best advantage: she was born for the spotlight. Equally as important as the photo was the message, meticulously scratched in a child's handwriting on the back of the picture postcard. There, when only ten years old, Helen composed her first poem:

Helen was a little girl
With many a golden curl
And her lovely eyes
Were as blue as the Summer skies
Oh no, I guess they're brown
So I will have to lose a crown.

By the time she reached her teens, Helen was blossoming into a young woman. She sat with her friends on the steps of the church across from Lorain High School, eating brown bag lunches and

As early as 1908, Helen (left) had the makings of a performer; Gertrude was more reserved.

Helen
Steiner Rice
Ambassador
of Sunshine

The Steiner sisters, Helen (right) and Gertrude, pictured here in about 1913, remained close all their lives.

making after-school plans. She "hammed it up" in front of the camera, borrowing the letter-sweater of a classmate for an impish picture. She fell in love—and tried to keep it a secret—writing a revealing verse at age fifteen that forms a wonderful bridge between Helen the child and Helen the young woman. Inscribed on a postcard dated July 4, 1915, the poem attempts to explain the power of love:

> *No one can guess*
> *Who I love best.*
> *No, never, never*
> *Even if you try for ever.*

The

Heart

Remembers

Vividly

For this beloved
Has oft been loved
And even loved
To be in love.
Love is a funny little thing
Composed of castles made of airy rings
But as to who I really love
I will not tell no turtle dove
For all to myself
My very own self,
I'll keep on loving
Hoping to in turn be loved
By one who is my own beloved

By this time, the "Honey Tiner" of Helen's girlhood was obviously growing up and attracting the attention of the young men at Lorain High School. One of them was Lewis Eugene Llewellyn, who was probably Helen's first real beau. While several years older, Gene was in the class just ahead of her at Lorain High School. The yearbook reported that he specialized at school in languages—Latin and German in particular—and, like many of his contemporaries both in America and Europe, was sufficiently fascinated by flying to want to become an aviator. Helen was as intrigued by Eugene Llewellyn's aspirations as she was by his broodingly handsome good looks.

Perhaps the best measure of the closeness between Helen Steiner and Eugene Llewellyn can be seen in the fact that all her life she saved the Christmas card he sent her, postmarked December 22, 1916. As greeting cards go—something Helen would come to appreciate keenly in the future—it was simple and unadorned. A postcard, it bore an indecipherable crest flanked by "MERRY CHRISTMAS" and followed by the message:

Helen
Steiner Rice
Ambassador
of Sunshine

Happiness is in the air
Merry Christmas everywhere
So I wish a lion's share
Of Xmas joy to you

It was signed simply "Eugene Llewellyn." While Gene Llewellyn must have played an important part in Helen's early understanding of romance, so too did William "Scoop" Dumont, the second of her early beaus.

Scoop and Helen were also high school classmates, participating in plays together and socializing frequently. He, too, was several years older than Helen, but was naturally drawn to her. Scoop was dismayed to find out he had to leave town on her birthday in 1917. He was sure her "host of other friends" would see to it she had a happy day, but he regretted he could not be among them. "I truly am sorry that I could not be here to see you tonight," he penned on a note enclosed in a tiny birthday card adorned with a butterfly, "but believe me when I say my thoughts will be of you and my wishes for a royal birthday during the long hours on the train." To commemorate the occasion in his absence, Scoop sent Helen a dozen roses, asking her to set aside one to remind her of him. "The other eleven," he wrote, "I dedicate entirely to the birthday of <u>THE BEST</u> little girl."

Their romantic involvement did not flourish, but throughout his years at Ohio State University and his long, successful business career, Scoop Dumont never forgot Helen Steiner or her "wonderful outgoing personality."

If Helen was popular with her friends, she was equally so with her teachers. Her favorite high school teacher, Edith Wilker, made an especially strong impression on the young and increasingly more self-possessed girl growing up in Lorain. Mrs. Wilker, like suffragette leaders around the country at that time, was encouraging a new generation of young women to focus their energies not only on securing voting rights, but also on entering the workplace, seeking college educations, and training for professional careers. Helen admired this teacher so much she remained in contact with her for decades. As late as 1955, Mrs. Wilker was still congratulating Helen for "advocating the cause of the ladies" and longing "to see just one woman of practical experience in a policy-making position" in the country. She also teased her former pupil, suggesting that perhaps Helen could become the "Carrie Anthony" of her generation, cleverly combining the names of the prominent feminists Carrie Catt and Susan Anthony.

Edith Wilker encouraged Helen in creative writing, which led Helen to submit her work to the high school yearbook, *The Scimitar*. The poem "April," filled with optimistic images, celebrated the spring of 1916:

> *April comes with cheeks a-glowing,*
> *Silver streams are all a-flowing,*
> *Flowers open wide their eyes*
> *In a rapturous surprise.*
> *Lilies dream beside the brooks,*
> *Violets in meadow nooks,*
> *And the birds gone wild with glee,*
> *Fill the woods with melody.*

By the time Helen wrote "Weaver of Dreams" one year later, it was clear to everyone that America would have to enter Europe's bloody war, a grim fact Helen expressed with deep feeling:

> *Weaver of dreams, come near I pray,*
> *Weave me a scene of childhood's day,*
> *Weave it slowly with touch so true,*
> *Weave it in every brightest hue.*

Weave it in outline clear and bold,
Weave it in colors blue and gold,
Weave it in happy girls and boys.

Photographs of Helen early in 1918 capture a wide range of personality and potential. In some snapshots, such as the one printed in the Lorain High School yearbook, she is demurely dressed, her hair carefully arranged, and her eyes full of belief in herself and confident of success in a professional career. Significantly, *The Scimitar* noted that Helen aspired to be a "Congress-Woman." Other pictures, in contrast, project an exquisitely femi-

Looking to the future, a serious Helen Steiner appeared in the Lorain High School yearbook, The Scimitar, in 1918.

The
Heart
Remembers
Vividly

*Her
exquisitely
feminine
and
reflective
side was yet
another
aspect of
Helen's
captivating
personality.*

Helen
Steiner Rice
*Ambassador
of Sunshine*

nine Helen Steiner; they portray someone who is reflective and aware of her own beauty, but respectful enough of lingering Victorian values to pose like a "Gibson Girl." Finally, there are photographs of Helen as a "Vamp" that were unabashedly modeled on the sultry, seductive posturings of Theda Bara—with the conservative, religious, and introspective Helen Steiner lolling on a divan, striking poses like every other teenage girl of the twentieth century who wanted to experiment and express herself.

At the same time that Helen showed so much to the camera, she also let her creativity range freely. Before her graduation, Helen wrote two final contributions to *The Scimitar*, one an ode of praise to her alma mater, and the other a short story, "The Screen Idol," that recounted the arrival at "Middleburg" [Lorain] of a matinee hero. Two girls, Betty and Byrd, exhausted their savings to attract the attention of "Earl Dorrance," but in the end their efforts were vain. Helen concluded the story with a line that spoke volumes: "Youth had lost its first illusion."

There were two stages of graduation from Lorain High School in 1918, an early one designated "A" and a later one designated "B." Whether or not someone was in the "A" or "B" class depended on when they were born and, to a greater extent, on how well they performed. Helen Steiner had always been an

Even when "vamping" as a teenager, Helen was photogenic.

exceptional student, so she was in the "A" class, scheduled for early graduation in January 1918. By then, she had grown into quite a remarkable young woman, one who felt confident about what she would do for the next several years. According to her plan, Helen would pursue a liberal arts course at Ohio Wesleyan, and then go on to study law at Ohio State University. Her parents heartily approved. Perhaps because of her early graduation, however, Helen decided to go to work before she began college. Less than a month after she graduated from high school, on February 1, 1918, Helen joined the staff of the Lorain Electric Light and Power Company, which later became the Lorain branch of the Ohio Public Service Company.

Helen's employment by the Lorain power company came through her high school home economics department. She had been recommended to the manager, Mr. Quillan, by a teacher. Quillan had asked for the name of someone who was creative, so the teacher immediately suggested Helen Steiner. Was she, he asked, willing to learn how to design and decorate lamp shades and then teach other women to do the same? At the time, the National Electric Light Association (N.E.L.A.) sponsored a three-month course in home lighting in Cleveland, and the company was willing to pay for the training. Helen, who needed to make some money before starting college, readily agreed. Upon her return from Cleveland, she was supplied with silk, braid, and fringe, and assigned a place in the front window of the company. There, Helen could demonstrate the art—totally unknown to her when she accepted the job—of lamp shade-making.

Her strong belief in the importance of service to others, indelibly imprinted on her by her father, made Helen Steiner and the Ohio Public Service Company a perfect match. When she took the position with the Lorain Electric Light and Power Company, the utilities industry was growing far more vigorously than anyone had predicted or expected. By 1918, consumers were beginning to awaken to the possibilities of electricity within the home, and the demand for household electrical appliances was skyrocketing. In 1918, Helen Steiner entered a service industry that was champing at the bit, full of unbounded enthusiasm, and receptive to fresh approaches.

When she first joined the utility, however, Helen's real aspirations lay elsewhere. "I began," she later told a reporter, "as a pinch hitter. I didn't do startlingly well at any of the jobs, but I did want to learn." This was, after all, supposed to be a temporary occupation. Along with her work, Helen continued to write, in 1918 typing out on company stationery a tribute to her mother, which she entitled "Life's Fairest Flower."

I have a garden within my soul
Of marvelous beauty rare,
Wherein the blossoms of all my life
Bloom ever in splendor fair . . .
Amid all this beauty and splendor,
One flower stands forth as queen.
Alone in its great dazzling beauty.
Alone, but ever supreme.
The flower of love and devotion
Has guided me all through my life;
Softening my grief and my trouble,
Sharing my toil and strife.
This flower has helped me conquer
Temptation so black and grim:
And led me to victory and honor
Over my enemy, Sin.
I have vainly sought in my garden,
Thru blossoms of love and light—
For a flower of equal wonder,

To compare with this one so bright.
But ever I've met with failure,
My search has been in vain—
For never a flower existed,
Like the blossom I can claim.
For after years I now can see,
Amid life's roses and rue—
God's greatest gift to a little child,
My darling MOTHER was YOU.

Helen seems to have grown unexpectedly fond of her job and coworkers at the utility company, for when the autumn of 1918 arrived, Helen did not enroll in college. Instead, she remained on the job in Lorain, and it was a good thing she did, for her life was soon struck by tragedy. A frightfully contagious disease, Spanish influenza, began to spread around the globe. No one was spared—not the soldiers fighting the Great War in Europe, nor the civilians who remained at home.

The flu, as it soon came to be called, permeated life in every settled, populous area of the civilized world. Newspapers everywhere reported the scope of the catastrophe, the growing numbers of dead, and ways to escape the disease. Along with everyone else, the citizens of Lorain, Ohio, braced themselves for the worst. At the beginning of October 1918, as the Allies were poised to strike a mortal blow against the Central Powers, influenza made its appearance in Lorain with sufficient fury to lead Dr. Valloyd Adair, the city's health director, to ask all physicians to report every case to his office immediately. Within two days, the *Lorain Times-Herald* carried a headline story that Dr. Adair had ordered the closing of all schools, theaters, and churches. Public gatherings were also prohibited, and Lorain High School was turned into a temporary hospital. The highly contagious Spanish influenza, while not fatal in itself, often made its victims susceptible to a deadly form of pneumonia. Many survived, but others were less fortunate. John Steiner was among the latter.

Helen's father was one of the first in Lorain to come down with the flu, taking to his bed at the house on Reid Avenue on October 3, 1918, after becoming ill on a railroad run. A strong, healthy, middle-aged man, his fate is testimony to the power of the disease. While he lay bedridden for two weeks, his strength ebbed, pneumonia set in, and nothing could be done to save him. He died on October 17, one of Lorain's earliest sacrifices to the disastrous epidemic that coincided with the end of the war in Europe. John Steiner's unexpected and untimely passing stunned his wife and daughters. Nearly a quarter-century later, on the anniversary of her father's death, Helen recalled the event in a letter to her mother:

> I know your thoughts will turn back to that day long ago when papa left us. The years go by so swiftly but the HEART REMEMBERS very VIVIDLY.
>
> I still remember that day—it was a warm very sunshiny lazy October day—I remember you sent me up to the store to get some ice cream because papa was going to try and eat a little. Isn't it funny how some little incident will leave an indelible mark that time can't erase.

The funeral for Helen's father was held at their home on Reid Avenue. Because of the epidemic, it was attended only by family and close friends, and Mr. Steiner was quickly interred at Elmwood Cemetery outside Lorain.

Word of Helen's loss soon reached Bill Sargent, a long-time friend from her school days in Lorain. Fighting in the trenches overseas, he wrote to her from "somewhere in France," expressing his "deepest sympathies and tenderest feelings" for Helen, her mother, and her sister. Then with the wisdom born of personal

2

*Living
and
Working
Enthusiastically*

elen Steiner's hopes of attending college vanished on the death of her father in October 1918, primarily because she promised her mother that she would support the family. Perhaps the weight of this new responsibility prompted Helen to rethink her attitude toward work, for after she had been at the power company for little more than a year, she approached the manager about a change in her situation. Helen asked to be trained as a bookkeeper. She recalled: "He was doubtful. Said it was work that didn't fit me at all. 'I know it,' I told him. 'But I want to learn. I know, too, that I'll detest it. However, detesting it will not stop me from learning the essentials of the job.'"

Eventually the manager relented, no doubt impressed by Helen's eagerness and determination. "He permitted me," she later recalled, "to have my own way and for a year I did little else, in my working hours, but master the essentials of bookkeeping. My, how it used to get on my nerves! I had determined that I was going to establish myself as more than 'a pay check.' . . ." After a year in bookkeeping, Helen had become "so enthusiastic about the company and its purposes that I thought of nothing else." She did not attribute her motives to anything more than the need to provide for her family. As she put it, "I was pretty selfish about it

Helen was a young woman who loved to take pictures as much as be in them.

all. I thought the more things I knew the more things I could do, and the more I could earn."

Meanwhile, Helen, the little girl who had preferred combing through encyclopedias to playing with friends, and preaching to adults rather than roller skating with childish abandon, was flowering into a young woman with an enormous love of life. The candid photos that fill her album unveil a fun-filled side of Helen that flourished with the loosening of social restrictions after World War I. Helen either personally snapped, or arranged to have taken, innumerable pictures of herself, John "Mac" McClendon, one of her early beaus, and their contemporaries, the Ohio Public Service

*Living
and
Working
Enthusiastically*

Helen's sense of fashion and love of hats is already apparent in this 1921 photo taken at the Cleveland Yacht Club.

Company office force. Other photographs recall picnics, sailing excursions on the Great Lakes (especially Lake Erie), and various adventures that carried Helen and her friends around northern Ohio—to Lakewood, Bowling Green, and Cleveland.

Years later, her sister Gertrude reminisced about a canoe trip in Michigan with a group of young people. At one point, treacherous waters required the party of friends to put ashore and carry the canoe overland past a rough spot. Helen insisted that she ride in the boat rather than walk along with the others, and, according to Gertrude, Helen was subsequently carried along while everyone else walked the portage!

One particularly revealing series of pictures from this early photo album illustrates the enthusiastic response the cheerful and

Helen
Steiner Rice
*Ambassador
of Sunshine*

vivacious young woman invariably elicited from others. On May 19, 1921, at least four young men sent flowers to remember her birthday, and Helen posed amidst the blooms, her slim arms full of flowers, the baskets overflowing. Graced with a beautiful, captivating smile, an engaging personality, and the determination to get what she wanted, Helen always managed, consciously or unconsciously, to become the main attraction.

At one point, when she had to contend with a bout of mumps, one of Helen's many young suitors was prompted to try his hand at verse in an effort to cheer her. Touched by the effort, her poetic soul responded to his sentiments. Helen treasured and kept his sincere and charmingly awkward effort, which read, in part:

On her twenty-first birthday, Helen received more flowers than she could carry.

*Gertrude
(left), Anna,
and Helen
(right) Steiner,
vacationing in
Bowling
Green, Ohio,
in July 1922.*

*Where is my little Helen?
Who makes my heart go thumps;
Why tucked up in her little bed
Nursing ugly mumps.
Poor little dumpy mumpy girl
She is my "bestus" friend.
I'd go the world around for her,
Her lumpy bumps to end.*

Helen
Steiner Rice
*Ambassador
of Sunshine*

That same photo album, which Helen carefully preserved for over half a century, also reveals a flair for fashion that remained with her all her life. Pictures repeatedly feature the young Helen bedecked with hats and parasols, scarves and fur collars—everything that was stylish as America moved further away from the Great War and into the Roaring Twenties. Yet Helen never went too far in her dedication to fashion; she favored a restrained, but tasteful style, which always included the distinctive hats that became her trademark. A former teacher once boarded a bus and, looking down the aisle ahead of her to see the back of a young woman wearing a hat, she remarked to herself, "Oh, that must be Helen." From the earliest days of her professional career in the 1920s until her death in 1981, Helen was famous for her hats!

While she was completing her apprenticeship as a bookkeeper, Helen devised a plan that combined her creativity with a steadily increasing knowledge of the Lorain Electric Light and Power Company. Once again, she went to her manager. This time, she asked for the chance to become a window trimmer, for she was fascinated by the marketing process and convinced that attractively decorated windows would be good advertising. In a time when the hearts of cities throbbed with people every day, her understanding of how a company should carry its message to the public was uncannily accurate. When interviewed by *Business Magazine* in 1926, she recounted the conversation:

"What do you know about window trimming?" the manager asked her.

"I know enough to believe that I can make our windows more attractive," was Helen's reply.

"Probably so," he responded. "But we have no appropriation for window trimming and you can't get very far in that game unless you can spend money on it."

Undaunted, Helen answered, "Let me use the stuff we have around here. I'll get a hammer, some nails, a saw, and some paint. That's all I need."

The supervisor remained skeptical, but began to yield in the face of her determination.

"Are you a carpenter—or, should I say, a carpentress—too?" he asked.

"I can trim the windows," was Helen's dogged rejoinder. By this time, the manager seemed to resign himself to his fate. He continued to question the persistent young woman, but only to salvage some remnants of bureaucratic control and personal pride.

"I have admitted that ability," he conceded. "But we can't pay you for doing it."

"I don't want anything extra, to start," she said in a compromising tone. "I just want a chance to prove that nice-looking windows will be a good advertisement. I'll prove their worth, in money, after I start them."

"I can't let you do it in regular working hours. You're needed elsewhere."

"I'll do it after working hours," she replied with determination.

"All right, all right!" the manager finally caved in.

Helen believed that the manager, who was obviously flustered by her insistence, expected her enthusiasm to wane. He was wrong, for like many who encountered Helen when she decided on a course of action, he underestimated her tenacity once she had committed herself to a plan.

No sooner had they finished their conversation than she began attending to the details of her scheme. Helen quickly changed the decorations in the two company windows framing the entrance. Both could easily be seen by the public. Furthermore, she photographed each display she used in the store's windows and began to enter the photos in nationwide window-trimming contests. At first, Helen met with disappointment. The judges ignored her radical approach to window design, but she persevered. In the end, Helen's patience and belief in her vision of carrying the company's message to the public paid off. One of her windows won second

Helen
Steiner Rice
*Ambassador
of Sunshine*

Helen's flair for decorating display windows won her national recognition.

prize in a national advertising competition. Ever the entrepreneur, she made sure that executives of the Ohio Public Service Company learned of her victory, and even though they were men who were unaccustomed to a woman trumpeting the company's virtues, they took notice. Shortly after her creativity and hard work won national recognition, Helen was promoted to advertising manager.

In her new capacity, Helen continued to create attractive windows and also began to write advertisements in prose and verse designed to educate the public on the advantages and conveniences of electrical power. She appealed to homemakers, showing

*Living
and
Working
Enthusiastically*

how the electrical home would improve their lives. In ads such as "Modern Babies," Helen put her rhyming talents to work.

> *Modern babies of modern days*
> *Require things done in the new modern ways,*
> *And so that each child may have comfort and rest,*
> *We wish to advise the "Electric" Way's best.*
> *With a Hoover cleaner to catch dust and dirt,*
> *Dear baby can play without being hurt,*
> *For the Hoover will get every germ in the rug*
> *And make baby's playground both comfy and snug.*
> *And then there's a washer to lessen the toil*
> *For mothers who wash all the clothes babies soil;*
> *An ironer to press out the wrinkles and folds,*
> *That baby's adorable little frock holds. . . .*
> *And do not forget baby's bond in this book,*
> *It's something you really should not overlook;*
> *We'll gladly redeem it, for we're trying to say*
> *"Hello Darling Baby"—the "Electrical Way."*

Like other public utilities at the time, the Lorain branch of the Ohio Public Service Company was encouraging the community to purchase its stock while simultaneously advocating the use of its products. Executives at the Henry L. Doherty Company of New York, which handled Ohio Public Service Company securities, learned about Helen's rhymed advertisements for the company and liked them. They contacted Helen and asked her to write some slogans that would encourage the sale of preferred stock. The result was an advertising campaign, late in 1923, which propelled sales of Ohio Public Service stock to a 500 percent increase over Doherty's previous endeavors. An example of her ads reveals Helen's understanding of the contemporary status of women. "A

Helen
Steiner Rice
Ambassador
of Sunshine

45

Merry Christmas for the Children" asked parents to consider the promising futures of their daughters:

> *Now Elizabeth Gene is just three months old,*
> *Her glorious future cannot yet be foretold,*
> *She may be a teacher of learning profound,*
> *Or she may devise some new beauty*
>   *compound,*
> *But nevertheless what e'er path she choose,*

She'll always be able some money to use. . . .
A few CS Bonds bought today for your Gene
Spells future prosperity and then that will
  mean
That she can go thru a fine college some day
And all of the money will be there to pay. . . .

With these efforts, Helen had suddenly become a saleswoman extraordinaire! From an ambitious lamp shade designer, she had risen to become an advertising star for the public utilities precisely when that industry was assuming an unprecedented prominence in American life. Reading of her merchandising success in the Doherty Company's news bulletin, the editor of *Electric Light and Power Magazine* contacted Helen, asking her to write an article on better merchandising methods in the electric power industry. The invitation produced another turning point in her career.

Helen's article, "Build Sales and Men: A Good Story of Constructive Merchandising," appeared in the May 1924 issue of the company's publication. Among the key ingredients for successful merchandising she endorsed was the precept that "The Noblest Motive is the Public Good." The article was remarkable not only for its outline of specific practical steps for creating window displays and good customer relations, but also for its presentation of an entire philosophy of life based on the author's own notions of service and positive thinking. Success in window trimming relied in large part, she contended, on "the ability and willingness to put oneself in the other fellow's place and think the thoughts of the persons or groups one desires to serve." According to Helen, the world of business needed employers who accepted something more than the delivery of the paycheck as their responsibility. They should also commit themselves to the improvement of humanity and the development of human resources. Helen concluded the article with a verse she had written that typifies her enthusiasm for life; the sentiments contained in the poem continued to be a mainstay of her life for nearly six more decades. She entitled it "Life":

If you would aspire a salesman to be
The rulings are simple and few,
Just work, be happy, and never forget
You're paid for whatever you do.
If you bargain with Life for a penny—
You'll find Life will pay you no more,
And you'll feel that you've failed completely
When you figure your final score.
If you realize Life's an employer
That pays you whatever you ask,
You'll learn to be honest and never deceive
In any performance or task.
So just set your wage at the highest stake,
And never give up in dismay
For any wage you may ask of Life,
Old "Life" will so gladly pay.

In 1924, Helen Steiner was among some thirty to thirty-five thousand women employed nationwide in the public utilities industry. Because of her rapid rise at the Lorain branch of the Ohio Public Service Company, Helen had garnered statewide recognition from the Women's Public Information Committee, a group organized by the National Electric Light Association to harness the power of its growing number of female employees. By 1924, her prominence led to Helen's election as Ohio chairman of this committee. In that position, she advanced the causes she believed in so passionately: the mutually rewarding nature of the connection between women and the public utilities, and the importance of women employees in conveying the message of the utility companies.

Helen even authored a pamphlet that dealt with the subject. Distributed at the WPIC geographic meeting in Cincinnati in the spring of 1924, her call urged women workers in the industry to make the most of this unprecedented situation: "Here is our opportunity to win for ourselves, something which is rightfully ours—A Place In Public Utilities. For remember, the activities of women in public affairs throughout the world are ever increasing in an amazing way." Ever the preacher, who as a little girl exhorted her audience to follow God's word, Helen's enthusiastic refrain focused on the importance of service. "No one has a greater opportunity to advance the interests of the public than we who are engaged in Public Service work. And of all the great opportunities—Woman's Is Greatest. Remember, [a] woman may be a small cog in the mighty mechanism that is turning the wheels of the electrical industry today—but she is a mighty one!"

Thanks to her remarkable success in the highly industrialized and populous state of Ohio, Helen was swept into the national limelight in the summer of 1924. Just when she began to make her mark, her home town, Lorain, was devastated by a tornado. Much of the city was leveled, power was cut off, many of Lorain's citizens were killed or injured, and the property damage proved to be an insurance agent's nightmare. An ice truck was blown into the showroom window of the electrical company just after Helen was named the winner of a *Forbes Magazine* prize for a story on "How Sound Public Relations Can Best Be Developed and Maintained."

Disaster turned into triumph for Helen. As Lorain clawed its way back from natural catastrophe, Helen was nicknamed the "Lorain Tornado." She was certainly cyclonic in the way she went about promoting the virtues of electric power, but the characterization also neatly captured a personality attribute that was to serve Helen well all her life. She was, quite simply, a dynamo, and she infected everyone around her with enthusiasm and optimism. During September 1924, for instance, Helen organized a team of eighty women who sold eight hundred shares of the utility company's preferred stock during a feverish ten-day campaign. Believing that the best leadership arose from example, Helen herself was responsible for the sale of 183 shares to forty-five individuals.

As she enjoyed greater and greater success in her projects, Helen Steiner became ever more prominent and popular. She used her prestige to maximum advantage, most notably by drawing attention to the importance of women in public utilities work, but also by underscoring their vital role in all areas of business. Helen, however, refused to depict men as adversaries. Rather, she preferred to view them as partners.

In "Woman—Electricity—Genius," an article she wrote for *Public Service Management Magazine* in 1924, Helen pointed out that: "Among men and women alike are to be found equal genius and equal intelligence," but "business men generally regard women as parsley trimmings on the platter of ham. . . . Blue eyes have, through the ages, been preferred to gray matter." She did not attribute these attitudes to maliciousness, but rather concluded that they were merely the result of unthinking tendencies to overlook the contributions of women. What women wanted, Helen asserted, was to "enter the electrical industry on an equality basis," to be partners and not decorations. With characteristic honesty, she summarized the problem in her distinctive style:

> Heretofore, even at best, woman had to fight longer and more persistently than man to be recognized and when after years she attained a measure of success, her recognition brought just about fifty per cent of the reward as that of a man having accomplished a similar amount of good work. . . . I hope that every utility company will give each girl employee a fair chance to prove that woman is a mighty and unconquerable force and an inestimable power in the

utility business today. The electrical industry needs the creative genius of women just as it needs that of men.

Furthermore, Helen pleaded with the men who ran the electrical industry to "take down all bars and offer complete participation in every branch of the work to which women are willing to employ their talents." In *Electric Light and Power Magazine,* she argued that "Women Have Won Greater Opportunity." "A woman employee, no matter how ambitious she is, cannot reach the percentage of co-operation best for the company if demonstrations of her ability are ignored, discounted or looked upon with indifference because of her sex. . . ."

To her credit, Helen was capable of seeing that what bettered conditions for women in the workforce would ultimately make things better for all, regardless of the business that employed them. Unconditional cooperation, not vicious competition, was the foundation stone of her vision of the future.

Helen's gift for self-expression and the enthusiasm she brought to her work soon captured the attention of the Ohio Public Service Company's leadership team. They were intrigued as much by her ideas as they were by the techniques she employed to express them. Assertive but compromising at the same time, Helen's approach confused the male hierarchy. It perplexed her superiors even more that Helen's physical appearance belied their notions that a woman in the business place always dressed like a man and affected masculine manners in hopes of achieving success. She was petite—not much over five feet tall—very pretty, and her flair for coordinating fashionable clothing maximized the effects of femininity and good taste. Despite her youth, Helen also had what her cousin Jane Steiner later described as a commanding presence. Jane perfectly captured Helen's effect on an audience when she observed: "If there were a hundred people in the room and she [Helen] walked in, she would be the absolute center of attention."

Soon, the forward-looking director of the Ohio Committee on Public Utility Information, Benjamin Ling, hit upon the idea of using Helen Steiner to represent Ohio's public utilities at the luncheon meetings of such businessmen's clubs as the Rotary, Kiwanis, and Lions. He took the suggestion to the general manager of the Ohio public utilities, who reacted with uncertainty. The general manager feared that Helen was too pretty to be taken seriously by businessmen. The two men finally compromised, agreeing to test Helen's approach and message before what Ling called "a friendly audience." They scheduled an appearance for her at the Ohio Electric Light Association convention at Cedar Point, a Lake Erie resort, in the summer of 1924. When interviewed in 1926 by *Business Magazine*, she recalled the offer:

"If you go over [i.e., 'succeed'] with your stuff it will mean more speeches," Ling told her. "I want to reach out and talk to business men all over the country," he concluded.

"I'd love it," Helen replied with characteristic fervor.

Impressed by her enthusiasm and confident in her ability, he ended their discussion by saying, "I want you to take on this job, as our representative. I think you can do it."

Facing this challenge as she did all of the other ones in her life, she did not disappoint her boss. As her first topic, Helen chose "Women as a Power in the Electrical Industry." She worked long and hard on her speech, trying to strike a balance between the principles she wanted to advance and the diplomacy that she knew would be necessary if her message were to have any hope of arousing sympathy and understanding.

The speech was a masterpiece. In it she argued that genuine public service required certain qualities that women possessed in abundance: patience, cheerfulness, sympathy, and tact. Helen knew what she was talking about, for she herself embodied those very attributes and several others that she did not mention. But what captured her audience most was the fact that she had an absolute

By 1925, Helen Steiner was a nationally known speaker who promoted the virtues of the public service industry and advocated the advancement of women in the workplace.

Helen
Steiner Rice
*Ambassador
of Sunshine*

command of statistics, showing precisely how, and in what degrees, the public utilities' efforts benefited their consumers. The combination she presented—beauty, poise, intelligence, passion, and command of her subject—astonished her first audience. It also made her an appealing and welcome addition to the speaker's circuit in an era when public speaking was a far more important part of social, intellectual, and business life than it is today. In five months she addressed more than twenty thousand people in the O.P.S. public relations effort to generate goodwill toward the utilities industry.

In speech after speech, Helen gracefully, but relentlessly, promoted the public utilities as among the best buys for consumers trying to get the most for their hard-earned dollars. While she was traveling, Helen continued to write advertising copy for the Ohio Public Service Company and the Henry L. Doherty Company. Living up to her claim as the "Lorain Tornado," she also found time to edit the O.P.S. newsletter, *Jazz Jumbles*. Unlike most company publications, it offered a fascinating example of Helen's humor and her efforts to infuse her coworkers with team spirit. In both prose and verse, she encouraged them to give their all to the sale of Ohio Public Service Company stock. To her credit, Helen also managed to toast the securities sales team:

> *Here's to the finest of all things on earth,*
> *Finest precisely and yet full of worth,*
> *One who gives service and loyalty too,*
> *One who in fellowship is staunch and true.*
> *Drink to him, toast him—do all that you can,*
> *For here is a toast to the DOHERTY MAN.*

Adept as she was at building self-esteem in others, Helen also knew the importance of self-promotion. She sent a copy of *Jazz Jumbles* to B. C. Forbes. He had just begun his odyssey to the top of the publishing world, but the magazine magnate knew talent when he saw it. Forbes responded warmly to Helen's initiative, suggesting that someone with her gifts was wasting time laboring on the shores of Lake Erie hawking the virtues of electric power and utility company stock. He replied, "The only place for you is not Lorain, Ohio, but some metropolitan city like New York where there is so much more room for doing big things." Flattered by the praise of someone she admired, Helen kept the letter, but she was not sufficiently moved to abandon her family and home and venture permanently to New York City.

Her success as a public speaker, however, took Helen far beyond the borders of the state of Ohio on a whirlwind lecture tour.

By the summer of 1925, this young woman in her mid-twenties had traversed most of the country alone, scurrying from California to Connecticut and back! The more Helen spoke, the more requests she received to feature her as spokeswoman at meetings and luncheons. Once she got a taste of performing for large audiences, Helen savored it, reveling in approval, watching nods of agreement, and receiving profuse congratulations and more invitations to address other groups than she could possibly meet. Helen was completely bowled over by the turn her career had taken. Later, she summarized this period of her life for the *Ohio State Journal* as "Breakfasting on obstacles, lunching on objections, dining on competition and feasting on prejudice." She had always believed in herself, but nothing in her life had prepared her to deal with such unprecedented achievement.

Public Service Magazine nicknamed Helen "Miss Demosthenes" after the famous Greek orator who learned to speak by filling his mouth with pebbles and addressing the ocean; the article's author went on to describe Helen as "one of the most popular and persuasive speakers of the public service industry." The *Denver Post* echoed that praise, hailing her as the "feminine electrical wizard of the country," one who intrigued audiences with her engaging personality, brilliant mind, and enthusiasm for her company and her work. By the time Helen had appeared to address a national meeting of electric railway employees, her fame had attracted the attention of the highest office in the land. She was invited to the White House to be photographed with President Coolidge.

Everything—far more than Helen had ever dreamed was possible—had gone her way. But she never lost sight of the ideals that had, at a very young age, led to make her a celebrity. As head of the Ohio Women's Public Information Committee, she was in a position to help other women, especially those who wanted to acquire the skills they needed to be successful public speakers, so she contributed to what she thought was a greater cause. She organized public speaking contests "to prepare our women to deliver the utility message in a clear, forceful, and effective manner." She also supervised the dissemination of a list of books and magazines that were designed to enrich the knowledge of those prospective public speakers. For her efforts, Helen Steiner was dubbed the "vivacious, guiding spirit" of the Ohio women's committee.

She was so successful in her work at the state level that she found herself appointed to the national committee in the autumn of 1925. Her commitment and energy did not fail her. She accepted the appointment and worked as feverishly as ever to meet all of its demands. Indeed, she gave so much of herself to the task that at one point Helen strained her vocal chords, which prompted her doctor to put her "on silence" for three weeks, and forced the cancellation of five speeches. There was, however, no stopping Helen's pen, or the sense of humor that worked its way into such timely public relations verses as "The Realtor's Lament":

> *The lot was grand; the house was fine,*
> *But there was no electric line.*
> *The yard was big and green the grass,*
> *But, oh, alas! There was no gas.*
> *The price was right, a splendid home,*
> *And yet there was no telephone.*
> *It looked supreme when viewed afar,*
> *But who could live with no street car!*
> *A house, a lot, a gorgeous place,*
> *But who could sell it in that case,*
> *For who would buy a modern home,*
> *Without electricity, gas, or phone?*

Throughout this dizzying period of her life, perhaps the most appealing attribute of young Helen Steiner was sincerity; she always practiced what she preached. By November 1925, when she wrote, "No man is truly great until he has learned the secret of serving his fellow men," she was well on the way to proving with her own life that true greatness and service were inseparably linked. "If we approach our civilization," she wrote in the *Lorain Times-Herald*, her hometown newspaper, "with the idea of selecting the greatest word in it, . . . one word naturally arises above all the other thousands and stands out supreme. . . . The Word is Service! Not service that serves self, for like lipservice that accomplishes naught, but Service in the true and intended meaning of the word—the service that labors in the interest of humanity—that confers an advantage, that benefits, that avails." One of the more fascinating aspects of the life of Helen Steiner Rice is that the more she emphasized service to others, the faster she rose to prominence herself.

Because of her work for the Ohio Public Service Company and other agencies, Helen found herself bombarded by requests to lend her talents to various charitable enterprises. One that especially touched her heart was the American Red Cross. When asked, she agreed without hesitation to become head of publicity and advertising for the 1925 American Red Cross drive in Lorain. Almost immediately after fitting this new responsibility into her routine, Helen saw a way to use her versifying skills in behalf of a call to membership in the organization she believed gave "the greatest, highest and most amazing service" in helping all humanity. Her ads were extremely clever, and when they were published in local newspapers, they told the Red Cross story in irresistible rhyme:

> *You've been asked to join the army,*
> *You've been asked to join a lodge,*
> *You've been asked to join a party—*
> *And perhaps you've tried to dodge;*
> *But now it is the "Red Cross,"*

56

Helen
Steiner Rice
Ambassador
of Sunshine

That asks you for your name
And surely you will join the ranks
That stand for "Service" fame.
It only costs a dollar
To be rated with the rest,
And when you join the Red Cross,
You've selected quite the best.
Your dollar keeps on working
Through this "mighty human hand,"
And you have the satisfaction
Of helping SERVE your land!

By the time she finished her tour of duty with the Red Cross, Helen seemed, to those who knew her best, to have "personality to burn." Harry Collins Spillman, widely respected author of a book on personality types, reported in 1925 that Helen exemplified the most effervescent and positive one.

She issued a challenge to others in a December 1925 *Public Service Magazine* article when she asked, "Why Not Super-Service?" After urging her readers to ever greater accomplishments, Helen then showed them the way to achieve the goals she outlined: "The pathway to all power lies through service, the greater the service, the greater the power. So, let us:

> *Do for our customers.*
> *Fulfill their requirements.*
> *Meet their demands.*
> *Anticipate their needs and*
> *Exceed their expectations in*
> *Our endeavor to develop a*
> *Super-Service System."*

Helen used her own unique brand of humor, tempered by a wholesome portion of common sense, to continue arguing the case for the working woman in speeches and magazine articles. "Why," she asked, "is a powder puff less legitimate in the presidential chair than a razor? Women are supposed to be the sex who attach more to what is on their heads than what is in them; but there is more tact in a woman's little finger than in a man's whole body." She continued, "One of the arguments against employing women is that they are merely going to work to tide them over until they are married. What inducement is held out to keep them from marriage, and what girl, worth her salt, wouldn't rather be married to a real man than to a telephone switchboard, or a cashier's desk or the controller in an elevator?" Women, according to Helen, wanted a chance to climb, to aspire. "Women don't succeed in business because men won't let them," she told an interviewer from *Business Magazine* in February 1926. In the vanguard of women's rights, even during the era of the "flapper," Helen contended that what women wanted was "the same right to cast our eyes on the manager's chair as have the men."

Considering all that she had accomplished and the widespread attention she had attracted to herself, it was only a matter of time before the Ohio Public Service Company's new advertising "star" was besieged by attractive job offers. Of the many that came, only one really appealed to Helen, for it meant that she could both improve her position and stay close to her family in Lorain. This new opportunity for advancement arrived in the form of a request that she become head of Cleveland Illuminating Company's public relations bureau. After discussing the pros and cons of the offer with her mother, her sister, and a few other confidants, Helen decided to move east to Ohio's largest city in March 1926. With great reluctance and a few tears, she announced her departure from the Ohio Public Service Company at Lorain with a farewell verse that veiled the pain of departure with humor; she called it "HELEN STEINER 'CRIES' GOOD-BYE!"

I've the queerest little feeling 'round the
    region of my heart,
And it keeps on getting "queerer" as the time
    draws near to part;
Just a steady little gnawing, just a
    quickening little pang,
Just a little lump that chokes me, as I say,
    good-bye, "Old Gang."

For the next year or so, Helen's job with Cleveland Illuminating allowed her to continue the public speaking she enjoyed so much, particularly to women's clubs, school groups, and business conventions. If she exhausted herself speaking to men's groups after lunch about such issues as allowing women to rise in business, she expended an equal amount of energy urging women to support each other in making the most of their increasing opportunities. In one of those speeches, "Eve Was Efficient—Why Shouldn't We Be?", Helen administered an unwelcome "dose of medicine" to her sisters in the workplace. "There are two kinds of women in the world," she claimed, "those who really want success and those who wish for it. The 'wanters' wade right in and fight for it but the 'wishers' seldom get nearer than the outer fringe of the battle and they are usually content to stand there and look with envy upon the heroes."

Ever fair-minded, what Helen found most upsetting in women was the cattiness and injustice they frequently displayed toward each other. She discussed it forthrightly in that same speech:

In my many years of work among women I have observed that every woman who rose to any great success, attained her goal through her ability to get along with other women. . . . When you hear a woman say that she wouldn't work for another woman for a million dollars, you are listening to the most efficient little grave digger in the world! She is not only digging her own grave but she is burying all the rest of us with her. If a woman has the brains to work herself into an executive position, boost for her—co-operate with her—help her climb still higher. For every time she goes up a step she leaves a vacancy to be filled by you—if you've shown yourself worthy. The women who go up are those who are sincerely interested in work and who work with their own sex.

Unless women go up as a sex, you do not go up! At least, you do not go up to stay. . . . As long as some women are underpaid and unrecognized you will be underpaid and unrecognized also. The line is not drawn between trades and businesses, it is drawn distinctly and firmly between men and women!

Helen was also a perceptive student of human nature. Years of selling electrical appliances had taught her that men and women in the 1920s approached purchasing decisions with very different agendas. She had learned that even when the man wrote the check and paid the bill, more often than not the woman actually decided what to buy. Helen believed that it was crucial for retailers and sales personnel to take into account the woman's interests when they marketed their products.

In an address to a convention of automobile dealers and distributors in December 1926, she told her audience that technological arguments alone could not sell a car to a woman. Style, luxury, and comfort were equally as important as engineering. Also, the personality of the salesman, his sense of humor, his patience in making explanations, and his courtesy were all factors that could influence a sale, for "consciously or unconsciously we human beings allow ourselves to make decisions not always on merit alone. . . . Believe me or not—if you cut out the 'extras' or eliminate all the inspirational and enthusiastic colorings in your presentation, you cannot reach a woman effectively." With this advice, Helen Steiner proved her prescience beyond any doubt. She had anticipated the importance of market research by half a century.

Yet, despite her successful professional life, Helen was torn by the same contradictory messages that 1920s society delivered to other women. While she argued for a woman's right to rise in any branch of any field where she felt she could use her talents, Helen also thought that there were areas in which women should not be employed. In one interview, for example, she told a Columbus, Ohio, newspaper reporter sent to cover a meeting of women in the public utilities field, "I don't believe in women being street car conductors or motormen or things like that." Also, like many other women of her era, she struggled with the issue of a woman's role in the home. She asserted without hesitation that women, if given opportunities to advance, "will stick to the end—and, the end is not marriage." But, when a reporter asked her if she believed in women continuing to work after marriage, she answered, "Writing or music, perhaps, but not public positions."

Helen later reflected on the implications of these and similar views that applied to her own personal life when she told a magazine interviewer, "If, in going around the country I find a man I like well enough, I'll marry him. And he needn't think I'm going to support myself, either!" Like most people, Helen was of two minds about important matters; she loved making the speeches and decisions that propelled her to prominence, but she still wanted to be transported in the canoe. She wrestled with how to reconcile these conflicting components of her personality.

The Helen who came into her own during the 1920s as a public relations expert delivered countless talks with a fervor that was more keenly appreciated during that era than any time before or since. "Do You Know Your Business, Or Do You Love It?" was one of her favorite topics. "If the world made work an experience of the soul—a romance of the heart, and not a loveless marriage of millions," she wrote, "what a fine old place this would be. . . ."

That uplifting attitude, she believed, was contagious: "When you have found the way to love your job—you will find a lot of people eager to possess the spirit that you will love to spread." Whatever else Helen may have felt in those years of growth from schoolgirl to public relations queen, one thing is clear: She loved her work.

She also believed in the people for whom she worked; she had given them all her trust, energy, and loyalty. Helen could only have felt betrayed when, in 1926, the leaders of the National Electric Light Association became embroiled in political and financial scandals that rocked the public utilities industry. Their self-serving deals, forged at the expense of customers and stockholders, made a sham of the message of public trust which Helen Steiner had so passionately articulated.

Their corruption and greediness shattered her idealism and left her feeling foolish for subscribing to a Christian work ethic apparently held in contempt by powerful and wealthy industrialists. Helen's baptism in the waters of harsh business reality proved to be another turning point in her life. It precipitated an inner struggle between the urge toward economic survival and belief in ethical propriety, a struggle that arose periodically throughout the rest of her long and fruitful life. She balanced the two forces remarkably well, but in 1926 moral outrage motivated her to leave the Cleveland Illuminating Company and open her own business.

Typically, she decided to resolve her inner strife in a positive way; she packaged her love of work, business principles, and enthusiasm for life into an individual enterprise. With the founding of the Steiner Service, a speaker's bureau operating out of Lorain, she hoped to be able to broaden her audience and deal with topics in which she believed. In the spring of 1927, Helen Steiner rose above the disgrace that was engulfing the top national executives in public utilities and struck out on her own.

3

'Til
Death
Do Us
Part

he "Steiner Service Brochure" announced Helen's new status. This clever pamphlet, produced and circulated by Helen, advertised her as a "Nationally Known Lecturer, Writer, Humorist, Pep-Talker, After Dinner Speaker, Organizer, Promoter, and Educational Director." She also scattered business cards as widely as possible, indicating that she could add "more pep, more power, more zip and more zest" to all occasions with her "snappy, scintillating and satisfying" messages. Helen's talents, of course, were already well known. The president of the National Broadcasting Company, M. H. Aylesworth, a former executive of the National Electric Light Association, had closely followed Helen's rise to popularity, and he was no less confident in her ability than J. B. Forbes had been. When, for instance, one of her articles appeared in a national women's magazine, *New Eve*, Aylesworth immediately wrote to Helen about her future plans. He also flattered her by suggesting, "I would like to keep in touch with you so that if anything opens up in New York I might have the opportunity of offering it to you." This was heady stuff for a young woman who, only a few years earlier, had held a menial job at a small midwestern power company.

At a time when a new car could be purchased for one thousand dollars and a family could live for a year on less, Helen's fees reflected her popularity as much as they did her self-confidence.

She began by charging fifty dollars plus expenses for talks at luncheons and women's club meetings. For after-dinner or banquet speeches and conventions, she demanded and received seventy-five dollars plus expenses. It is testimony to her skill and renown that, in a very competitive market dominated by men, she was able to double her fees within a year!

During her first year as an entrepreneur, Helen charmed audiences of all sizes, ranging from corporate conventions where the air was thick with cigar smoke to ladies' luncheons that oozed catty civility. Regardless of the group she addressed, Helen continued to work her magic. She always struck sympathetic chords in her listeners. Her appearance before the Massachusetts Mutual Life Insurance Company offers a perfect example of how well Helen could connect with her audience. After her talk, despite the fact that she knew next to nothing about the industry, she received a letter from E. W. Snyder, a general agent, urging her to enter the insurance business. He was so taken with Helen and her message that Snyder assured her she could become not only "one of the most successful woman underwriters in the country," but also "one of the most successful underwriters among <u>all</u> underwriters."

The chairman of the board of the Dayton Savings and Trust Company, William R. Craven, heard such good reports about the "Lorain Tornado" that he wrote to Helen in June 1928, inquiring about her availability for an engagement. He wanted her to deliver an after-dinner talk to the Dayton Clearing House Association, a prestigious organization made up of the directors and officers of five local banks. The bankers, Craven explained, planned to have their golf tournament, followed by a dinner, on June 27, and everyone wanted "a speaker who will have a subject that is peppy and full of humor." Recounting many dismal experiences in the past, he emphasized that "All of our previous talks have been long, serious and heavy subjects, and this time we want something light and entertaining."

This was a challenge perfectly suited to Helen's tastes and talents, and because she was subsequently approached by Dayton's Rotary Club to speak at their meeting on the same day, the possibility of combining two speaking engagements interested Helen. Perhaps it was because she felt a certain regional loyalty, or maybe she was just captivated by the banker's enthusiasm, but Helen agreed to give a talk before Mr. Craven's group for $150 plus expenses, a fee substantially discounted from the $200 she normally received! It was a decision that would profoundly change her life.

Eager to please his guest, Mr. Craven arranged to have the bank's trust officer, a young, handsome bachelor named Franklin Rice, chauffeur Helen to and from the festivities at the Dayton Country Club. Franklin was also assigned to act as her escort for the day. Helen arrived at the country club with Mr. Rice, not at all nervous at the prospect of talking to captains of industry and lions of society. She had, after all, spent several years entertaining precisely this kind of group across the country. Helen gave one of her favorite talks, "Living and Working Enthusiastically," and during it she issued several challenges. She urged the seventy men at the meeting to make a romance of their vocations, to love their jobs, not just know about them. The *Dayton Herald* reporter who covered the event described her talk as "humorous and sparkling," but more remarkable was the reaction of the roomful of stiff-backed bankers. They so enjoyed themselves that they voted to schedule another gathering before the end of the season. Helen's triumph was complete.

At the end of the evening, Franklin Rice offered to take Helen out for a late dinner before escorting her back to her hotel in his shiny new Cadillac; she agreed. During a pleasant meal, they exchanged small talk about the day and he promised to save any newspaper clippings about her speech. Miffed by his apparent ignorance of her stature, Helen informed him that she was accustomed to front page stories; she expected the local press to give a thorough report on her talk. Helen thought Franklin was rather meek; in fact, he was overwhelmed.

Thirty-four-year-old Franklin Rice, a shy and reserved man, was smitten. Helen's speech and their subsequent dinner had taken place on a Wednesday evening. The next morning he cancelled his engagement to Bernice Chrysler. By the following Sunday, Franklin Rice had traveled the two hundred miles—no mean feat in 1928—to Lorain, Ohio, so he could personally deliver the newspaper reports praising Helen's Dayton appearance. He arrived for his first formal visit in a chauffeur-driven limousine.

In the beginning, the attraction was more pronounced on Franklin's part than on Helen's, but she soon began to return his interest. During the following two months, they spent a great deal of time together. Franklin drove to meet her whenever possible. He called her as often as he could, and they talked on the telephone for hours. They also corresponded regularly.

Helen soon learned more about this youthful officer of the Dayton Savings and Trust Company and just as much about his prominent family. Franklin Dryden Rice was the youngest of the three children born to Franklin Rice and Mary Victoria Dryden. Franklin, his brother Elwood, and his sister Catharine animated the impressive Rice house on Grand Avenue overlooking the valley of the Great Miami River. In earlier years, the elder Rice and his wife had operated a profitable family farm in Montgomery County and participated in the Zion Memorial Church in Moraine. Later, Franklin's father turned to the agricultural implements business, moved his family to Dayton, and became a distinguished and prosperous businessman.

Young Franklin Rice could not have helped but notice that success surrounded Helen Steiner in the same way it seemed to encompass his older brother Elwood. Ambitious and serious even as a boy, Elwood Rice had, at a very young age, parlayed his father's unpatented wall-plaster formula into a fortune by supply-

Franklin Rice trained as an aviator during World War I, but the conflict ended before his squadron saw active duty.

Helen
Steiner Rice
Ambassador
of Sunshine

ing wall-plaster to the large office buildings and apartments in Dayton. In 1902, at the age of twenty-three, he pioneered advances in the electrical sign industry, which resulted in yet another fortune that arose from his contribution to the advertising industry. Elwood then moved to New York to oversee his growing empire and once ensconced there founded the *Rice Leaders of the World,* a by-invitation-only public relations organization that included the nation's most influential advertisers.

Although fifteen years his brother's senior, Elwood Rice's personality and success had a profound effect on Franklin. Franklin's older sister, Catharine, also felt the impact of Elwood's victories as keenly as did Franklin, for she left Dayton as soon as possible. She married Edgar Appenzellar, and afterward they resided in Philadelphia.

By the time Franklin Rice met Helen Steiner, he had established himself professionally, despite the fact that he operated in his older brother's shadow. His preferred image of himself, however, and the one he most eagerly shared with Helen, dealt not with his years as a banker, but with his military service during World War I. The newspaper clippings he saved and showed to Helen detailed his ground school training at Ohio State University and the University of California at Berkeley, instruction at Camp Dick in Dallas, Texas, and assignment to Wilbur Wright Field in Dayton. In August 1918, Lieutenant Rice had been ordered overseas for duty as a night bombing pilot in the Handley-Page aircraft then used in France. Much to his disappointment, Franklin never experienced combat. The Armistice was signed in November, before his unit was ever called upon to mount a raid.

Franklin Rice presented an imposing picture at the wheel of his Cadillac.

Honorably discharged from the Army Air Service, Franklin contacted his old employers at the Dayton Savings and Trust, and he was welcomed back into the company family. In the unprecedented growth period following the Great War, Dayton Savings and Trust prospered and expanded like virtually every other company in America. Franklin Rice benefited from the company's success, moving up the banking ladder until, by 1928, he had become a vice president of the bank, overseeing its trust functions.

Franklin pulled out all the stops in his courtship of Helen Steiner; here, at last, was something he could do on his own and do well. He invited Helen, her mother, and her sister, Gertrude, to meet his mother and join them for an outing on Lake Erie aboard a private yacht, the *Juniata*. Anna Steiner declined the invitation, for though she approved of Franklin's interest, she was worried that Helen might get hurt. Helen and Gertrude, however, were more excited; they eagerly boarded the *Juniata* for a weekend on Lake Erie. The *Juniata* cruise and Franklin's lavish displays of attention cemented the relationship between Helen Steiner and Franklin Rice, which grew ever stronger as the summer of 1928 turned into autumn. By the time Franklin joined the Steiners in Lorain for Thanksgiving dinner, many serious conversations had occurred about the future, and that special holiday was indelibly marked for Helen when he gave her an engagement ring.

Helen brought an enthusiasm to her prenuptial arrangements that rivaled the force and excitement of her successful speaking assignments. She hid Franklin's ring from nearly everyone save her mother, sister, and a close friend and neighbor, Isabel Bloedorn. Helen always had a sense of the dramatic; waiting for the right moment, she elected to announce her engagement formally at a bridge party that was given in her honor on December 5, 1928, by her sister and Isabel.

The importance of this new turn in her life can best be seen in the way Helen worked on the individual notices, personalizing the

folders for each of her guests. Helen adorned the announcements with yellow silk ribbons, and then embellished them with silver hearts featuring her name and Franklin's. Within each beribboned envelope, she placed a photograph of the newly engaged couple, and laid the folder in a pink and yellow box. Pleased with her cleverness and the effect she expected to create, Helen wrote exuberantly to Franklin the day after Thanksgiving:

> I have been working like a young beaver on my announcement folders and boy oh boy they are beginning to look sweet. I am tickled too

[sic] death with the effect, and I don't mind the work at all since they look so pretty. I love to do things that make you proud of me—you know I would probably kill myself working on something just to hear you say "gee that is great."

As creative in their own right as Helen, Gertrude and Isabel enameled metal house numbers in pink and yellow for the bridge tables, purchased rose and yellow baskets and filled them with candies for table favors, and then decorated Isabel's house with yellow chrysanthemums, pompoms, and pink cyclamen. On Thursday, December 6, newspapers in Lorain and Dayton announced the engagement of the nationally known lecturer and writer to one of Dayton's foremost businessmen.

Almost from the first moment she saw him, with his fancy clothes, expensive car, and lofty title, Helen worried that she and Franklin came from very different social backgrounds. Anna Steiner had reinforced this notion with her talk of the Rices being from a higher social class. In reality, both families had grown from agricultural roots, and while the Rices enjoyed greater wealth, nothing else distinguished them. Nevertheless, Helen felt socially inferior to Franklin and lucky to have someone with his credentials seriously court her, so she made every effort to please him. Though she tried to mask her feelings of inferiority, Helen occasionally let them show. When, for example, she designed a special Christmas card at the time of their engagement, Helen felt obliged to explain it to Franklin and seek his approval:

> I decided that you wanted me to have "classy" Christmas cards and I owed it to you if to know [sic] one else to send out some that you would be proud to say I created. . . . I feel better just cause I am going to send them to some of your friends and I want to make you proud of me and the way I do things. I owe that much to you—I know you appreciate every effort I make to do little clever things.

Still, there was enough pride of independence—perhaps a bit of the rebel—in Helen to keep her from being too much of the humble, obedient bride. Though she wanted with all her heart to please Franklin, Helen resisted his attempts at intrusion into areas she viewed as fundamental to her self-reliance. One such domain was her finances.

In fact, her opposition to suggestions that Franklin begin to manage her funds may have been behind what he referred to as their "first fuss," a quarrel on Thanksgiving eve, just prior to the announcement of their engagement. Helen later asked him to forget "how naughty I seemed to be Wednesday." Still, she continued to balk at proposals to alter insurance policies on her mink and squirrel coats, and expressed uneasiness over a scheme to "borrow on what 'our' stock may make." In the end, her desire to please Franklin overrode her initial reservations, for in the weeks before their wedding day, Helen gave in and agreed to let Franklin handle her stock portfolio. Neglecting to tell her until after the fact, Franklin soon sold Helen's Ohio Public Service stocks—the first securities she had ever owned.

The engaged couple's clash over stocks presaged a more profound disagreement between them. Insecure in his masculinity because of his "younger brother" role, Franklin rejected from the outset the image of Helen as an astute, successful businesswoman. He insisted that she be his "darling baby child," and left no doubt about his feelings concerning the relationship between man and wife. Just before their wedding day, he wrote her about the financial transactions he had completed using Helen's resources, assuring her, "I will not let a nickle of your money get away and you just remember that, darling. . . . You have enough worries packing, so just let me handle this matter, dear."

Nevertheless, Helen eagerly looked forward to her marriage, and she was deeply offended when a close friend confided that Franklin's character "dimmed by comparison" to her own. Reporting the slur to Franklin, she wrote: "She don't [sic] know you are a hundred times more wonderful than me. . . . If she knew how 'smart' you were I bet she would tremble with shame." Helen disclosed that she had sent a sample of Franklin's handwriting off—a common practice in the 1920s—to the same graphologist who had rendered a complimentary assessment of her own, but she rejected the analyst's personality profile of her fiancé without telling Franklin the details of what was evidently a negative assessment. "Well, she is a dumb bunny—by gosh—we can do better than that ourselves," she wrote to him, concluding with a biblical allusion: "Anyhow we don't believe in the writing on the wall or any place else."

Predictably, Helen, and Franklin for that matter, made the most of their approaching wedding. Friends of both the bride and groom eagerly joined in arranging the prenuptial festivities, and parties in Lorain and Dayton honored the pair. A "hearts and flowers" motif set the tone for a dinner party in Lorain where the more daring guests read original poems in the form of toasts to the bride-to-be. Similarly, Franklin's friends in Dayton orchestrated a bachelor party and several formal affairs, culminating with a dinner for bank officers, company directors, and their spouses at the home of the president of the Dayton Savings and Trust Company. The marriage of a Rockefeller could scarcely have had more social activity surrounding it.

From the beginning of their relationship, Helen had taken pains to cultivate a good rapport with the members of Franklin's family, writing frequently to them, apprising them of plans, describing her trousseau, and generally doing her best to generate a spirit of goodwill. Franklin's mother, Mary Victoria Rice, responded warmly to Helen's initiatives, good-naturedly teasing her even as she offered friendly advice: "you must be sure 'Boy Blue' sees you good before each promenade or he will not know his dainty bride with all the different changes." On a more personal level, she added, "I am just as thrilled as a girl . . . because [I am] so intensely interested." "Mother Rice," as Helen called her, believed, with the wisdom that only mothers can claim, that Helen had made Franklin happy from the first day they met.

Those sentiments were echoed by Franklin's niece, Evelyn Appenzellar. She had never met Helen, but she extended her affection in a revealing letter. "It seems quite natural to be writing to you," she offered from distant Philadelphia, "and altho [sic] we have never met, I have seen and heard enough wonderful things about you to feel that I am indeed a lucky girl to be getting such a 'pal and friend.' Then too, you must know Franklin is very dear to me and I can't help loving you for bringing him so much happiness."

These and similar expressions of support and understanding encouraged Helen, leading her to think that she had not made a mistake in tying her fortunes to the fate of the Rice family. But there was something that made Helen think that she was an unworthy addition to the Rice empire.

Franklin's brother, Elwood, was the source of her uneasiness, for he seems to have been less receptive to her than the other Rices. Helen attributed his disdain to her lack of high social standing. She was undoubtedly correct, for Elwood reveled in his fortune and status. He was given to opulent displays of wealth. On one occasion he hired a private train, "The Elwood Rice Special," to transport family members to a party. He undoubtedly believed that his cleverness had won him both treasure and the right to be commander-in-chief of the Rice clan. Elwood was also accustomed to getting his own way. He was determined to control the wedding arrangements. He usurped the bride's traditional prerogative to have the wedding in her hometown and church, and insisted on paying for a lavish New York society wedding that Helen's family simply could not afford.

In his own way, however, Elwood tried to welcome Helen into the family. Writing from his "Nido," the somewhat pompous name he gave his "pheasant's nest" suite at the Plaza Hotel, in Decem-

*Helen and
Franklin
were guests
of honor
at a dinner
given by
Franklin's
brother the
night before
their wedding
in January
1929.*

Helen
Steiner Rice
*Ambassador
of Sunshine*

ber 1928, Elwood lectured Helen: "You know what a wonderful young man you are getting in Franklin . . . with your loving inspiration his excellent career will even be more fruitful."

His churlishness notwithstanding, Elwood Rice planned and hosted an elegant dinner in New York City honoring his brother and prospective sister-in-law the night before their wedding. Fifteen guests, all formally attired, gathered in the Plaza Hotel's "White and Gold Room" for dinner and dancing on the evening of January 29,

1929. Elwood supervised the most minute details. Menus inscribed with the Rice family crest were specially printed for the event, which featured entrees of lobster Americaine and roasted Canadian partridge. Most of those present were members of the Rice family, but the chairman of the board of Franklin's bank and his wife also attended in honor of Franklin. Gertrude Steiner was the only one of Helen's family and friends present. The New York City and Lorain, Ohio, newspapers agreed: this affair was "one of the most attractive and important dinners of the mid-winter season in New York."

As her wedding gift to Franklin, Helen ordered a specially made platinum wristwatch. She mailed it to him in Dayton a few days before their wedding, and he put it in a safety deposit box at the bank until his departure for New York. "I never had anything so valuable or so darling," he wrote her, "and from the sweetest person in the world. Darling every time I look at the time all the rest of my life I will think of you instead of what time it is." Franklin reciprocated with a gift to Helen that was also a platinum wristwatch, one inset with sixty-six diamonds. Not to be outdone by Franklin, Elwood Rice gave his sister-in-law a diamond brooch featuring fifteen large diamonds highlighted by eighty small round ones set in platinum.

The wedding took place on Wednesday morning, January 30, 1929, in the drawing room of Elwood's "Nido" at the Plaza. The room was lavishly decorated with roses, Easter lilies, palms, and ferns arranged upon an altar set before the fireplace. Dr. Daniel Poling, pastor of the Marble Collegiate Church, performed a brief ceremony that was witnessed by the small group of family and friends who had assembled for dinner the night before. Helen's wedding ensemble featured an orchid crepe dress with an embroidered cape, complemented by a felt hat and gray shoes. Her corsage was a tasteful blend of orchids and pink sweet peas. Eager to please her new family, Helen wore the watch from Franklin and the brooch from Elwood, who served as his brother's best man.

Gertrude Steiner was her sister's maid of honor. Following the wedding, breakfast was served in an atmosphere of lively conversation amidst a profusion of flowers.

Helen had designed her own wedding announcement. Modeled on a standard marriage certificate, it highlighted pictures of Helen and Franklin, indicating the date and place of their marriage. Each announcement was enclosed in an envelope—here Helen's creativity shone—which depicted their honeymoon cruise itinerary on a map. It also notified friends when the couple would be at home in Dayton.

By noon on January 30, Franklin and Helen Rice were safely aboard the S.S. *Columbus*, ready to depart on their honeymoon cruise around the Caribbean. Flowers, fruit, candy, nuts, radiograms, and telegrams from well-wishers saluted their union as the *Columbus* sailed out of New York harbor. Elwood Rice sent the newlyweds two huge baskets of flowers and a wedding cake. Franklin's colleagues, the officers and directors of the Dayton Savings and Trust Company, sent a basket of flowers, and the company's travel department asked the ship's staff to decorate the honeymooners' cabin with serpentine confetti, balloons, rice, and a basket of fresh vegetables. When Helen Steiner and Franklin Rice began their married life in the winter of 1929, it seemed a storybook beginning.

Yet the world of opulence Helen had entered made her uneasy. Aboard ship, she encountered a continuous stream of theme parties, celebrations, and fine dining. Then, when the S.S. *Columbus* docked at a seemingly endless number of ports—Trinidad, Havana, Curacao, Panama—in the Caribbean, Helen was forced to confront the poverty, hunger, and squalor that marked the lives of the islanders. Franklin had brought a satchel full of gold coins with him to throw from the ship to the natives who would swim out to meet it. The cities, streets, homes, and children of the poor were frequently the subjects of snapshots Franklin Rice took for a honeymoon album, and often he photographed Helen surrounded by

The newlyweds honeymooned in the Caribbean. Trinidad was one of the ports where their luxury liner docked.

In every Caribbean port, Franklin Rice photographed Helen with native children.

Financial troubles were the last thing on the minds of the honeymooners returning from their cruise in February 1929.

'Til Death Do Us Part

sad-eyed, eager groups of native children. Her winning smile and fashionable attire provided a sharp counterpoint to the stark background. She was disturbed by the contrast.

Franklin and Helen apparently saved every scrap of memorabilia from that cruise. Their treasure trove included informational brochures, place cards, menus, and everything else that could be classified as a souvenir, including the first valentines they sent each other while still aboard the ship. All of it went into their honeymoon album—even an invitation sent to friends after they returned to come and see their home movies! By the spring of 1929, even the most casual observer could only conclude that Franklin and Helen Rice were well on the way to a lifetime of luxury and wedded bliss.

When Franklin and Helen settled in Dayton, the city was enjoying a period of boom in manufacturing and population growth. Franklin's bank, the Dayton Savings and Trust Company, had just celebrated a quarter-century of service to the people of the city. The company boasted in its silver anniversary brochure about "steady, splendid growth," and featured the photo of Franklin D. Rice, head of the Trust Department. In an advertisement carried by a local newspaper, Dayton Savings urged businessmen to follow the growing trend of appointing the bank as executor or trustee of their wills. Such recommendations could only redound to Franklin's credit.

Franklin preferred this optimistic outlook to the ominous financial signs that had trailed him even on his honeymoon. When he received telegrams aboard the S.S. *Columbus* that stock market conditions were unsteady, he encouraged the bank to continue buying securities. Franklin Rice was only one among the many active speculators who did so. Helen had expressed concerns to him before their marriage about borrowing on anticipated profits—buying "on margin" as it is now known—but Franklin had ignored her warnings in the belief that the economy would stabi-

Friends decorated Franklin and Helen's house on Grand Avenue in Dayton to welcome them home from their Caribbean honeymoon.

lize. His faith in the future and confidence in his talent for reading the market led him, imprisoned in a trap of his own making, to continue risky purchases despite mounting losses. Long before he realized the danger of his position, the stock market plummeted in October 1929. When it did, Franklin first viewed the "crash" as an aberration; then, as time passed, he slowly began to realize that a disaster far beyond his comprehension had occurred. Unbelieving, Franklin did his best to make some sense of his shattered life, but the task was too great. His bank's assets, as well as his own, disappeared far faster than they had accumulated.

By the end of December 1929, Franklin Rice, who less than a year earlier had thrown gold coins to naked children in the West Indies, drew up a financial statement listing cash assets of only $1.23. He owed money for groceries, coal, insurance, travel, and clothing, and to add to his misery, the Dayton Savings and Trust Company closed its doors, leaving him unemployed. The bank was eventually reorganized as the Union Trust Company on

*'Til
Death
Do Us
Part*

February 25, 1930, but its regeneration was of little more than academic interest to Helen and Franklin Rice, for the bank no longer listed Franklin among its officers and employees.

In a matter of weeks, Franklin Rice had gone from the top of the mountain to the bottom of the valley. In an effort to keep creditors from repossessing the Rice family home, Elwood Rice offered, in April 1930, to assume the monthly mortgage payments. Franklin had purchased the house at Elwood's insistence anyway and from the outset had relied on one hundred dollars a month from his brother to support it. Still, the burden of maintaining the huge house remained with the hapless couple. Elwood's proffered help and the accompanying stipulations produced what Helen later called a "reign of terror," something which left them with "a lot of hurt feelings—sore and bleeding hearts and misunderstandings."

It was not in Helen Steiner Rice's nature, however, to wallow in self-pity. She had spent most of her adult life preaching optimism, enthusiasm, and perseverance to her audiences, and this was no time to abandon her beliefs. Confident that she and Franklin could overcome any obstacles fate placed before them, her only worry was a practical one: How could they save Franklin's pride and pay the bills at the same time? After weighing her options, Helen decided that her husband's pride would have to take a back seat to survival.

Helen naturally drew on her past success. She reopened the Steiner Service that had been closed little more than a year earlier, and once again sent out her brochures, pasting stickers with her married name and Dayton address over the old information. Nearly all of her public talks were designed to combat the negative feelings of the Depression era. In March 1930, for instance, Helen delivered a pep talk at the Springfield [Ohio] Kiwanis Club entitled "Up-and-At-'Em." In addition, Helen and a friend advertised themselves as contract bridge counselors. In an era when playing bridge was a national mania, these two women let it be known that they were willing to teach group and individual bridge lessons, using their Dayton homes as studios.

Helen publicly assumed the most optimistic outlook possible, but at home her situation was steadily growing more desperate. Weeks passed and Franklin remained out of work, old debts continued unpaid, and new bills were added to them. At Christmas, Helen "recycled" the gifts others had given her and sent them to Franklin's mother and sister so that the Rices in Philadelphia might have a happy holiday. In time, Helen was compelled to devise a "last resort" plan that would make it possible for her to become the full-time breadwinner and still spare Franklin's feelings.

Mindful of Franklin's pride and eager to avoid unfavorable comments, Helen hoped to persuade everyone that she had decided to renew her "urge for a career." She calculated that if she moved to the East Coast and went to work for Ernest Rice, Elwood's son, she could live quietly with Ernest's mother-in-law, Minnie Coward, and make enough money to pay the debts she and Franklin had accumulated in Dayton. Ever the positive thinker, Helen hoped that she could pull off "a ruse to camouflage from the public and my own dear precious mother and sister my dire circumstances and my constant suffering and turmoil."

Helen's innocent and well-meaning idea precipitated a furious response from Elwood Rice, who phoned her from New York, viciously ridiculing his sister-in-law as a "silly little pep talker" and branding her as a "sneak who wouldn't be tolerated." Since it was totally unexpected in both content and fury, Elwood's harangue left Helen "on the verge of a nervous collapse." The outburst had a beneficial effect, however, for it convinced her that the time had come for some straight talk with Franklin's older brother.

Helen sat down at her typewriter on January 22, 1931, and responded to Elwood's diatribe, typing across the top of the page:

"PLEASE READ EVERY LINE CAREFULLY AND RETAIN LETTER FOR I NEVER EXPECT TO STATE THESE FACTS AGAIN." Pointing out that she had tried, from the first, to handle the whole situation tactfully and delicately, Helen then put sentimentality aside:

> I'm tired of this stupid stalling and quibbling—courageous people don't do it—I want utter frankness and I intend to state things in a form that cannot be further misunderstood. . . .
>
> What I have <u>suffered</u>—<u>tolerated</u>—<u>endured</u> and <u>done</u> for the <u>NAME OF RICE,</u> in the two years I have carried that name, is more than I have ever done for anybody, collectively or individually. I am being more <u>honest</u> with you than anyone else has ever been but I hardly expect any credit for that. People prefer "<u>Applesauce</u>" to <u>honesty</u> anytime!

In spite of his financial assistance, Elwood's disregard for Helen's feelings hurt her deeply. "If I had a copy of all the tirades and ruthless declamations you have hurled upon my innocent head I think even you would agree that there is a limit to even an angel's patience and endurance," she wrote. "I <u>appreciate you</u>—<u>admire you</u> and <u>love you</u> for the many splendid things you have done but I can't see why you spoil the wonderful effects of your goodness by such wild tirades that avail nothing."

Helen proceeded to discuss the main financial burden she and Franklin faced—the house at 713 West Grand Avenue, which Helen characterized as "an expensive white elephant." Ever the realist, she called on Elwood to face the facts:

> Elwood, be honest with yourself—Didn't you insist on keeping 713 open? Didn't you insist on us living here to maintain appearances and didn't you figure in your own heart that it was a measure of necessity with you? The public figures this is your house anyway and you didn't want it to be <u>sold at a sheriff's sale</u> for <u>non-payment of loans and taxes,</u> to save your <u>name</u> as much as anything.

Even with Elwood's financial assistance, Helen continued, she and Franklin could not pay for heat, taxes, interest, and repairs.

> We had $5 between us and starvation when you finally sent us that last $50 which is gone about now. . . . This house is an <u>obligation</u>—we do not live here by choice neither do you <u>support</u> it by choice—it is an unfortunate circumstance for which no one is directly responsible I guess.

Helen pleaded passionately with Elwood to understand, respect, and take into account her feelings and her concern for Franklin's deteriorating state of mind.

> <u>Nobody</u> in God's world wants to see Franklin working more than I do. It means <u>my life</u>—<u>my future happiness</u>—I have everything at stake—to you it means only <u>material things</u>. Your "necessity" as you term it is measured in dollars—mine in heart throbs. There is NO comparison—so please <u>never act as though</u> I was <u>not doing</u> all in my power to get him back into harmony with his being and re-established.

She could not afford, she argued, to let her own spirit be crushed, for then she would be of no use to Franklin. She allowed that Elwood was under pressure "from all sides and sources," and yet, she continued, "life metes out to us pretty much what we bargain for ourselves." She concluded by acknowledging Elwood's generosity and goodness, while reserving her right to have her say: "I want you to take this letter as I have written it—fairly and with not a grain of animosity in my being."

In the end, however, Elwood prevailed, for Helen and Franklin remained in the house on Grand Avenue. Helen accepted a speaking engagement before the Masonic Temple's Noon Tide Club, of which Franklin was a member, the week after her exchange with Elwood. Her presentation was billed, in language charmingly typical of the era, as a "tip-top tingling talk," one that would "relegate to the shade 'Old Man Grouch's' lamentation . . . that business is poor and getting poorer, and times are hard and getting harder, and living [is] tough and getting tougher." Whatever comfort Helen Steiner Rice may have given to others, the lamentation in her advertisement also precisely described everyday life in her own home.

On Helen's birthday, May 19, 1931, Franklin was still out of work. The picture of melancholy, he daily sank further into the pit of despair, mostly because his pride made it impossible for him to accept the fact that he could no longer support the household. Still, evidence of Franklin Rice's optimism—his hope for a better tomorrow—can be seen in his relationship with Helen. At the darkest time, he sent her a humorous, if bittersweet, birthday letter lamenting their financial situation:

> To my Bunny:
>
> You've often heard of Dollar a Year Men but you never heard of Dollar a Year Women. Well here and now I dub and create you one and may you continue to add age and prosperity to your already many charms. . . .
>
> Again I say—the best for you is none too good although we are "out of that brand" just now we are expecting some in shortly. Can you wait????
>
> With many good wishes for a very Happy Birthday with abundant love, hugs and kisses I still remain, although busted,
>
> Your devoted "fritz" and husband,
Franklin

As the summer of 1931 wore on into autumn, the Great Depression gripped the country in a way that no one had ever experienced. Franklin kept waiting for something to break in the banking industry, and Helen, for her part, accepted offers to speak and taught contract bridge classes. By October, she had developed a plan that would coordinate her need to purchase playing cards with an opportunity to make a merchandising suggestion to J. R. Gibson of the Gibson Art Company in Cincinnati. Helen had once met Gibson through a friend, Gibson sales manager Sam Heed, who had worked for years in the utilities industry. Heed and his wife had befriended Helen when she was in Los Angeles for a speaking engagement. Subsequently, when Helen visited Heed in his Cincinnati office, he took the opportunity to introduce her to his boss, J. R. Gibson. She was hoping that Gibson remembered her.

Helen recounted their first meeting and her current financial state in a letter she wrote to him on October 22, 1931. She didn't complain, but explained that she had been reduced to teaching bridge lessons. She asked for a small favor. Could she buy playing cards in quantity direct from Gibson Art and then sell the cards to her students, thus bypassing the retailers who ordinarily handled the cards in Dayton? J. R. Gibson's response to her request was sympathetic and cautiously positive.

While he was not averse to Helen's suggestion about playing cards, he seemed far more interested in a plan Helen alluded to at the end of her letter for improving the merchandising and public awareness of Gibson Christmas seals, which then were sold almost exclusively in department stores. Excited by Helen's proposals, Mr. Gibson invited her to come to Cincinnati and meet with him and Sam Heed.

She arrived in Cincinnati and had a preliminary conversation with Sam Heed and J. R. Gibson. Their suggestions were so far from what she expected that they sent Helen's mind "somersaulting at the rate of a thousand revolutions a minute." Gibson and Heed asked her to become a troubleshooter for the Gibson Art Company. Aware of her background and talents, they wanted Helen to evaluate their various markets and make recommendations on overhauling the presentation of their "Everyday" and "Holiday" lines of merchandise. To sweeten the proposition, they suggested that she only commit herself to a trial assignment in Pittsburgh, where she could begin as soon as she could make arrangements at home. If everything worked out satisfactorily, Helen would then join Gibson Art as a full-time employee. She asked for some time to discuss it with Franklin before making a decision.

Recognizing the plan as an answer to a prayer she had not dared to utter, Helen nevertheless was mindful of its likely impact on the rest of her life. After some consideration, she wrote cautiously to Sam Heed on November 20:

> I have not ceased to ponder, deliberate, analyze, consider and re-consider every angle of the problem that confronts me. . . . I am convinced that I should accept your offer and I am confident that I shall find satisfaction and contentment in this work and that in time it will bring me back into harmony with the laws of my being. However, my life right now presents many angles—it is tangled and intricate and since coming home I realize that I cannot walk off into a new world with the same ease one orders a chocolate soda.

For one thing, there were commitments she had made. But a more important, and certainly more difficult, consideration revolved around how she would break the news of her new undertaking at home. Understandably worried about the implications of such a major decision, Helen apologized to Sam Heed for what she called "the jumbled state of this letter," noting that:

> It was written amid a state of confusion and hectic happenings but I did not want to make you wait for an answer until some remote moment when I could compose my rattled brain cells in temporary quiet and peace—a letter written under those circumstances might be a long time in coming.

Despite her trepidation, Helen knew that she and Franklin were in no position to decline such a generous offer as the one tendered by the Gibson Art Company, for it was clear that the

Great Depression was not a temporary problem. She began to prepare in earnest for her departure from Dayton, eager to relocate in Cincinnati and become "at least a 'step-child' of the 'Gibson Family'" as soon as possible. By mid-December 1931, Helen had accepted Gibson's offer, gone through a brief training period in Cincinnati, and taken a train to Pittsburgh, where she found herself trying to learn all she could about the greeting card business in the midst of the Christmas selling season. Helen was understandably overwhelmed by her ignorance of this field, but so far as she was concerned it was like window decoration; she knew little about it, but there was nothing to prevent her from mastering it.

Fortunately, Helen did not have to face this uncertain future alone. Sam Heed reassured her that he, J. R. Gibson, and others at the company would give her the time and help necessary to "get you educated in our business and [make you] able to stand on your own feet and do a constructive job for us." Her first paycheck from Gibson Art, a welcome addition to the Rice's empty bank account, was mailed December 31, 1931. Another was promised in mid-January. The alliance with Gibson Art seemed, in the nation's gloomiest of times, to carry with it the promise of a better year—or at least the hope of respectable survival—for the Rices. Mr. Gibson himself told Helen that the company had done a brisk business in spite of the Great Depression, and was likely to increase its profitability in 1932. He expressed full confidence in her abilities and encouraged her, noting ". . . the business is not very difficult to know and in a year's time you will feel like an old timer."

When she first accepted the job with Gibson, Helen planned to return to Dayton for Christmas. As she looked into the future, she realized that a temporary, or perhaps permanent, move to Cincinnati early in 1932 was something she and Franklin would have to face. She proposed closing the house at 713 Grand Avenue, but Franklin resisted. In an effort to forestall the threat this rapidly changing situation posed to their relationship, the young couple worked out a plan they hoped would reconcile Helen's good fortune with Franklin's pride. After much discussion, they agreed that she would pursue a full-time career with Gibson Art Company, while he waited for something to break in Dayton. In the meantime, Helen would move to Cincinnati and Franklin would drive down every weekend. It was awkward, but at least they could spend Saturdays and Sundays together. In January 1932, Helen Steiner Rice took up solitary residence in a downtown Cincinnati hotel.

The first trial balloon of this new arrangement was flown on Saturday, January 30, when Franklin drove south on the Cincinnati-Dayton road to pick up Helen and take her home so they could spend the weekend together in Dayton. It was their third wedding anniversary. Both Helen and Franklin did their best to make the most of a difficult situation, carrying on their usual friendly banter and behaving as though nothing were out of the ordinary. For Sunday dinner, they went to a Chinese restaurant—Helen was especially fond of chop suey—and recalled with bittersweet snatches of conversation their wedding day in New York City three years earlier. Afterward, Franklin drove Helen back to Cincinnati, and on Monday she left for a two-week business trip to Detroit. Before they parted, she gave him instructions on what needed to be done regarding maintenance of the Dayton house. Hurt, and feeling that their proper roles had been reversed, Franklin wrote glumly to Helen's mother and sister:

> Well guess you will be surprised to hear from "Old Man Rice" but Mrs. Rice has instructed me just what to do and so I am doing it pronto! . . . Enclosed are two checks "which Gertie is to cash at once" as per usual instructions. . . . I suppose that Helen writes you the news—what little there is, so all there is for me to say is what Eddie Cantor said last night on the radio:

Now I lay me down to snore,
Insured for 50 thousand more,
If I should die before I wake,
My wife would get her first good break.

As it turned out, Helen had already had a good break with the job offer from Gibson, and she was doing everything she could to make a success of it. She worked like a Trojan. With the same fervor that had accompanied her whirlwind speaking tours of the 1920s, Helen traveled to Washington, D.C., Baltimore, New York City, Newark, Boston, and other major cities for Sam Heed during the spring of 1932. A consummate salesman, Heed wanted Helen to advise him on problems of merchandising, distribution, and employee efficiency, matters that were natural for Helen, since she had a knack for evaluating the accounts, sales representatives, and policies of the Gibson Art Company. Heed wrote to Helen at her hotel in Philadelphia, concluding with a witty reference to the children's game of "Tag":

> . . . I want you to keep your ear to the ground and really help me find a solution to some of our problems. I have had plenty of people go around and come back and tell me what conditions are, but I am looking for somebody who can help me whip the situation. Tag, you're it.

Even before he employed her, Sam Heed had a great deal of confidence in Helen's abilities. He had observed her at work in the utilities industry when he served as vice president of the Union Gas and Electric Company in Cincinnati, and later as president of the Electric Household Utilities Corporation in Chicago, so when she came to Gibson, he was confident in entrusting her with a highly confidential position. She reported directly to him, sending detailed and classified assessments of her findings in each city as well as her own recommendations for improvements. Heed was especially concerned about a loss of business in New York City, and was delighted when Helen reported, "we must set the Hudson River on fire." He had just placed a promising new executive in New York, and expected Helen to help the young man revive Gibson's sales there. "I wish you would make it your business to ask enough questions in the New York Office to see whether or not anybody in that office knows what it's all about," he urged.

Helen applied the same eager and energetic outlook to the greeting card business that had won her praise in the world of public service. Her enthusiasm was infectious. The owner of one Gibson outlet in Rochester, New York, summarized her impact on all who met her. After Helen had visited him in March 1932, he wrote a letter of praise that dubbed her the new "Ambassador and Sunshine Go-Getter" of the Gibson Art Company. "What a great line the Gibson Art Company would be able to promulgate thru your enthusiasm, your million dollar smile and personality," he exclaimed. "Oh Boy! I can only say that Sam Heed is sure some picker, and has a very valuable assistant that he cannot well afford to do without," was his conclusion.

Helen's accomplishments in her new job at Gibson made Franklin's inability to find work, much less regain his former status, all the more galling. His mother wrote to Helen shortly before her birthday, sending money, "lots of love," and a savvy evaluation of her youngest son's condition:

> Here comes the best wishes in the world for the sweetest daughter in the world, to have the happiest birthday in the world, on Tuesday and all the days of your sweet life. I am wishing you health, wealth, and happiness. Now there is just one thing would make you happier than that! and I hope big boy gets it real soon. Aren't I good at guessing? . . . the best is none too good for you.

"The best" did not, however, come to Helen on her birthday. On the contrary, May 19, 1932, dawned with Franklin Rice named in a lawsuit that accused W. E. Hutton, the brokerage house he dealt with, of making illegal transactions. The *Dayton Daily News* carried the scandal on the front page. According to the lawsuit filed by the state superintendent of banks, Hutton had knowingly allowed Franklin Rice to open and maintain private brokerage accounts for illicit purposes using the funds of the Dayton Savings and Trust Company. The suit alleged that, over a period of years, Franklin had been permitted to buy, sell, and trade various stocks through three different accounts. Furthermore, he had carried on the transactions without the bank's knowledge, and, most damningly, without using his own name. The suit sought a judgment of $181,466.50 from the brokerage house, which was liable under state law, but no direct charges were filed against Helen's husband.

Franklin's situation not only tested the Rice's financial stability; it also measured their faith. In her birthday letter to Helen, Franklin's mother expressed the hope that her son and daughter-in-law would go to church sometime, noting that it ". . . would make me happy to know it, and you would feel better I know, my dears. The longer you stay away the harder it is to get started." At this time in their lives, however, the basic issue for Franklin and Helen Rice seemed to be survival.

If Franklin Rice's circumstances seemed bleak after the stock market crash, they had now deteriorated well beyond his comprehension. With Helen away all week, he had no one to talk to; he occupied himself doing the errands she suggested, filling in the time between her weekend visits. Franklin struggled to overcome the crushing burden of melancholy. When he wrote to her on August 4, he reported that he was going to visit friends that evening: "I don't know who they have invited, but I will get my sandwich just the same I guess." All the while, he kept pursuing leads for work, and at one point he revealed to Helen that he was especially hopeful about a new scheme:

I am feeling much better and have the old pep back now for I am sure things will break out on the upside for us now. This is a new idea and plan altogether but not a waiting around process like the other was. Will tell you all about it Saturday and I know you will be pleased to pieces that I have done what I did and it is "wind-up" or the "run-down" of the whole business.

On Labor Day weekend, 1932, Helen came home to celebrate Franklin's birthday. She found time to arrange a surprise by decorating their house with birthday cards. Aware that Franklin was particularly vulnerable, Helen did everything she could to remove any doubts he might have about the unqualified nature of her love. She gave him neckties, suspenders, hose supporters, and a cash gift of five dollars so he could buy a new hat for the autumn. Afterward, they joined several friends for a makeshift picnic. Everyone brought what they had and shared it. Although Franklin never suspected what was afoot, his friends combined the picnic with a surprise birthday party, complete with cake, candles, packages, and the gift of a pet kitten. "We had lots of fun," he later wrote to Anna and Gertrude Steiner, "and I enjoyed it all so much and thought it was nice of them to go to all that trouble for me. . . ." He closed with this happy thought: ". . . the depression don't [sic] seem to have hit the 'birthday business' at 713 Grand."

While Franklin, despite his bravado, floundered in Dayton, Helen's fortunes steadily improved as she developed recommendations to revitalize the Gibson greeting card lines. Her observations were taken seriously at the home office. In less than a year, she was able to prepare a comparative analysis of Gibson and its competitors, and in August 1932 she submitted an evaluation calling for major changes, including the elimination of many "parasite" lines. If Sam Heed was looking for a reinvigoration of the entire company, he got it from Helen Rice. "Smaller and Smarter" summarized her prescription for greater success and the development of a "compact, clever, concentrated line." She reported to Heed:

> Our Line today lacks snap, style, and real clean, crisp, sparkling humor. . . . We can expect bigger volume from few numbers, and it will not be necessary for the good numbers to carry along the slow movers. . . . Concentration on a smaller line of rapid movers would pep up sales considerably and we would sell more cards at less cost per card, and with less expenditure of time, energy, and money to the company and salesmen. . . . A smaller line with rapid turnover of designs would enable us to put our new, clever ideas before the public while they were still "original models."

It was also a forward-looking Helen Rice who recommended in 1932 that Gibson enter the gift-wrapping market in earnest, for she saw it as a promising area with little serious competition except for the Norcross Company. And Helen knew that if Gibson hoped to succeed in this new area, they would have to change their tactics dramatically, a view she made clear in a letter to Heed: "Presenting our present line of papers against Norcross is like entering the ring to meet the maddened bull with a candy cane for a sword." The "gift dressing" market, she predicted, "is rapidly developing to a greater degree each day and if we once decide to go into this with a vengeance we could easily make it a paying line." Recalling her early days as a window trimmer, Helen advocated that Gibson concentrate on visual displays, for, as she wrote in developing her argument, "Actual display stimulates buying more effectively than any other method. If we want to sell that cellophane ribbon, try styling it on boxes for store display!"

Professionally, things could not have been going better for Helen. The skills and advice she brought to Gibson had already been noticed by other companies, and General Electric, among others, approached her with a job offer. By the end of September, an executive in New York wrote and suggested she come to what was then known as "Gotham," where she could easily land a nationally syndicated newspaper column and radio job as well. Though she was flattered by the attention, Helen told the eager promoter:

> I know it will be hard to believe but at present I am pretty happy right here at the Gibson Art Co. Of course, I am no longer able to claim the distinction of being the highest paid woman in the industry as of yore, but I do get a lot of soul satisfaction out of my work these days. There is a whale of a job to be done here and you know I adore tackling hard, tough things. If I really do the job right I feel confident that the Gibson Art will not be unappreciative of my efforts. . . . I seem to have found here a bunch of people I really enjoy working with and you know heart finds do have intrinsic value after all.

Ironically, while Helen was turning down job offers, Franklin was failing in all his efforts to find work. He realized that he had to become "adjusted to the new order of things," but at the same time felt that nothing he had ever experienced equipped him to make the transition. Disoriented, he still did his best to pursue employment opportunities. On Tuesday, October 4, 1932, he wrote to Helen's mother and sister from Richmond, Virginia, where he had gone "to meet some men on a proposition." He reported that their proposal, which focused on a new investment business, looked promising. Returning from Richmond, he picked up Helen in Cincinnati for their weekend together, and showered her with details about a brighter future. When Franklin dropped her off at the Gibson Hotel in Cincinnati on Sunday, October 9, Helen believed that her husband was looking forward with optimism to the unfolding of this new prospect.

Helen went to work at Gibson Art on Monday, happy for what she thought was Franklin's impending success and eager to develop her ideas for an expansion of the company's product line. She began to feel uneasy, however, when she returned to the hotel on Tuesday and found no letter from Franklin. Assuming he was wrapped up in his new project, she wrote a humorous note:

> <u>No Letter!</u> How Come??? Gosh you're either so almighty busy you can't find time to write the "old mamma"—or else you don't have a three cent stamp—Gee—ain't that "something"! Well, I can't figure it out—but then there's lots of things I can't "figger" out. . . .

The more she thought about his silence, however, the more her inclination toward good-natured teasing gradually turned into alarm. By Wednesday evening she still hadn't heard from Franklin, so Helen decided to telephone him. She dialed his number repeatedly throughout the evening, but each time there was no answer. Her mind racing, Helen worried one minute that something terrible had happened and the next talked herself into believing that she was fretting needlessly. As the hours passed, her concern for Franklin's safety won out. She phoned his friend, Chalmers Miller, who had not seen Franklin since the previous Saturday. She then tried, unsuccessfully, to reach Charles Coleman, another of her husband's closest friends. By now, Helen's deepening concern had turned to dread, but she still managed to keep her composure and write another letter late Wednesday night:

> Gee, dear—I can't imagine what happened! If you're sick, I want to know—Gee, this is "<u>Awful</u>"—and don't ever get me so excited again . . . I've been to my P.O. box ten times but still no mail—

Finally, in desperation, Helen called Chalmers Miller again and asked him to search for Franklin in the house and grounds on Grand Avenue. Miller found Franklin's body Thursday morning in the garage behind the Rice home, slumped over the steering wheel of his LaSalle. Unable to contend any longer with the strain of his circumstances, he had returned from Cincinnati, looked into the future, and decided that it held no place for him. Franklin drove his car into the garage, closed the door, and breathed in the carbon monoxide fumes. He was dead in a few minutes, but the car continued to run until its fuel was exhausted. In the pocket of his coat, Franklin left a note identifying himself, and asking that his wife be notified in Cincinnati.

Just before he took his life, Franklin wrote Helen a long letter. It was dated Monday, October 10, 10 A.M. He simply could not continue to rely on loans to cover living expenses, he explained, and he had used every last cent of available cash to go to Richmond. To add to his misery, his most recent letter to Elwood, asking his brother for seventy dollars to help him through the crisis, had not been answered. Desperate, he soon reached the conclusion that his death would serve a useful purpose, for it would ease the financial burden of supporting him. Franklin concluded the letter by asking Helen to repay the money her mother had loaned them, and to help support his mother during the remainder of her life. Rejecting sympathy, he wrote:

> I have often told you that I was not going to go down, and down and down and become a common bum, and I won't either. When my money goes, which it has I too, must fade out of the picture, as I must go down with the colors at the top of mast and the band playing. No one up until now knows the terrible hard conditions under which I had been trying to get along, trading this for that and switching this into that to get money just to live from day to day.

Yet, despite his bitterness over the hand fate had dealt him, Franklin wanted to make sure that Helen knew how important she was to him, how much he loved her:

> The most enjoyable time of my life has been the weekends that I had to look forward to with you and how I did enjoy them. Darling I love you more than anything and hope this one last error I am committing will be forgiven. . . .

Always try to remember that I am trying now even to do what I think is the best, to remove myself from the scene to allow other things to become adjusted and so that the pity that I seem to excite can be eliminated and happiness soon again rule the lives of my loved ones. . . .

Darling, my love, remember me as the happy go lucky, care free boy of 1928, when I was driving to Lorain to see you, and the "Aviator" [see earlier photograph] which you have in your room at the Gibson.

Helen was at work when she received word of Franklin's death. There was no opportunity to absorb the shock privately. Franklin had been a prominent businessman, and Helen herself was well known. Just as she feared, a newspaper reporter stopped her as she left the Gibson Art offices and asked her for a comment. She refused. A front-page headline announcing "Franklin D. Rice Ends Life" ran in Thursday's *Dayton Daily News*, while the Cincinnati and Lorain newspapers carried detailed stories of the suicide.

The next day Helen returned to Dayton to make funeral arrangements. Her mother and sister caught the train down from Lorain to support Helen in this awful time of picking up the pieces. In his final letter, Franklin had urged her to rely "on your old true and time tested friends." He believed that once she became adjusted to his absence, she could "return to work with a new viewpoint on things, I hope one not restrained with the thoughts of an unhappy and struggling husband." A tragic figure, whose presence filled only four years of Helen's long life, Franklin might seem to have been but a footnote in Helen Steiner Rice's maturation and success. Yet her brief relationship with him touched her like nothing else, and while his death brought to a close a tumultuous chapter of her life, it became for Helen the most significant event in the shaping of her future.

4

True
and
Time-Tested
Friends

*f*ranklin Rice was buried near his father in the cemetery of the Zion Memorial Church in Moraine, Ohio. It was an unimaginably painful time for Helen, who struggled to find clues that would help her understand the meaning behind this unexpected loss. She gradually mustered the strength to confront both the emotional and financial turmoil occasioned by Franklin's death. It wasn't easy—far from it—but Helen was sustained by her faith in God's benevolence, her fighting spirit, and a memory of the Franklin Rice who had sat with her on top of the world for a few months during their brief married life.

She decided that the best way to remember Franklin was exactly as he had asked—as a dashing young World War I pilot. To one of his former business associates, Dr. D. A. Scheibenzuber, she wrote:

> . . . to me he typifies a real hero for it took the same courage he had when he flew a bombing plane during the war—to walk out there to that grim, cold garage and die when he had so much of life before him and everything in the world but "money" I guess. All the disillusionments, disappointments, discouragements and struggling of the past years is erased now—and I go on honoring him—respecting him and loving him.

But even while she wrote courageous letters and talked to confidants matter-of-factly, Helen's brave exterior belied her inner despair and turmoil. She could only work through her own agony and heartache privately, venting it as poetry in her verse diary:

> *I don't want money*
> *I don't want fame*
> *I don't want to add*
> *Any laurels to my name*
> *I don't want to travel*
> *I don't want to "drink"*
> *I don't want to read*
> *I don't want to think*
> *I don't want to eat*
> *I don't want to walk*
> *I don't want to sing*
> *I don't want to talk*
> *I don't want to "get"*
> *I don't want to give*
> *I don't want to die*
> *And I don't want to live*
> *But though life is perplexing*
> *I've gotta live through it*
> *In spite of the fact*
> *That I don't want to do it.*

Friends and relatives tried to console Helen. Her mother and sister provided one base of support. So, too, did many of her coworkers at Gibson Art Company. But Helen also found touching consolation from an unexpected source. It came from Minnie Coward, one of Franklin's relatives by marriage, who had been a widow for many years. Minnie was especially fond of Helen, and her compassionate letters brought her the greatest comfort. Writing with the authority of experience, Minnie told her:

> . . . you will find he will live closer to you now than ever. It is hard to tell you this now in your first sorrow, because I know The Old World looks so grey, houses all seem to need paint, the sunshine isn't even bright & nothing matters, we go on just automatically thru habit hardly knowing what we are doing, but time is a great healer. . . . God always fits the back to the burden and gives us strength to go on & no matter how much we mourn nothing brings them back no matter what we do—and I think our bravery at this time is then reward. . . .

"Mother Minnie," as Helen fondly called her, also told her adopted "daughter" that Elwood Rice was "more than crushed" by the death of his brother. According to her report, things were so bad that he had "become ill." In a shrewd assessment of the contrast between the two brothers, Minnie confided that Franklin had always had friends and was loved, but Elwood led "a lonely life." She also pointed out that Elwood, too, had suffered financially from the Depression, but unlike Franklin, he had received sufficient help. Minnie concluded by expressing a fear that if she wrote her real thoughts about Franklin's suicide to Elwood, "he would almost feel compelled to act likewise." Ironically, Minnie wrote that it was Helen who was sustaining Elwood, as well as Franklin's mother, and "Elwood is appreciating you as never before."

Minnie Coward's fundamental advice was both wise and irresistible. She told the grieving widow to put herself first for a while: "Your great sacrifices have been made & you owe something to <u>yourself</u> as <u>no one else</u> would put themselves out for you—and after all—you have been thru your suffering, and nothing broadens more." Much as she appreciated "Mother Minnie's" counsel, Helen struggled in her grief to understand if love had been worth the price it exacted. Her diary reflects her anguish:

Yes, I was a SUCCESS
I was BELOVED
I was ACCLAIMED
I was ADMIRED
I was RESPECTED
The world knew me and I knew the world;
I gave it up for LOVE because LOVE is
worth its PRICE
LOVE makes up for all losses—LOVE
overshadows all????
But now
I am a FAILURE
I am UNLOVED
I am ALONE
I am DEFEATED
I am NOBODY—I have NO ONE
I am DELUDED—DISILLUSIONED
  and DEJECTED
LOVE COULD NOT PAY its debt.

Helen's mind told her that when people take their own lives, it has nothing to do with the actions of others, but her emotions made her feel responsible for Franklin's death; she asked herself over and over again if she could have prevented it. As time passed, she concluded that while she might have done more to ease Franklin's pain, she was only a victim of his death, not the instrument that caused it.

Steeled by "Mother Minnie's" warnings about the difficulties she would face during holidays, the young widow fought off depression and mustered the courage to compose a special Christmas greeting in 1932. Even though the card's decoration was in keeping with Christmastide, its sentiments told all her friends how much she appreciated their support in her time of tragedy:

Christmas this year cannot be a happy one for me, but the charm of the day with its message of peace and good-will brings comfort.

And remembering folks like you softens my sadness and brings a glow of warm friendliness about me.

So may your Christmas in every way be filled with loveliness and may the coming year be just a bit sweeter and more kind, is the wish of

Helen Steiner Rice

During the period of Franklin's financial difficulties, Helen tried to deal with their circumstances forthrightly. Now that she was faced not only with the emotional devastation of his suicide, but also with unpaid bills, those honest and decent sentiments helped carry her through the emergency. Most of their possessions, except those Helen took with her to Cincinnati, were sold at auction to defray her husband's staggering debts. She resolved to satisfy Franklin's remaining creditors out of her earnings at Gibson Art. Helen's powers of organization and belief in financial responsibility served her well. By the end of 1933, she had repaid Franklin's most pressing note—the one from the Merchants National Bank and Trust Company in Dayton.

As the hurt eased, she realized that her pain was not an enemy to be feared, but a blessing that made her more aware of the dimensions of human suffering. Helen expressed new appreciation of life's vicissitudes in a letter to one of Franklin's friends:

If I die tomorrow . . . while I am only 32, I can assure you that I have lived a hundred years or more. But sorrow makes us more tolerant and I am of the opinion that if we never had trouble we would never find out how really nice folks are in this tough, hard old world of ours.

As she gradually pulled herself out of debt and depression, Helen told that same friend that even though everything she had in the world was now gone, she was determined to make the most of her situation:

. . . I am not complaining for I have my health and I still look upon work as a great adventure that nothing can destroy—for friends may fail us—fortunes may shrink—success is but fickle and yet if we have learned to love and respect work and found in it adventure and romance we have something that neither time nor space can rob us of.

Helen threw herself into analyzing Gibson Art's marketing efforts. Soon, her proposals brought sweeping changes to the merchandising techniques of the Gibson Art Company, and eventually her advice was translated into a program that emphasized service and awareness of customer needs.

Helen was also called upon to use her skills as a motivational speaker to reinvigorate the Gibson sales force. She espoused the same themes in talks to salesmen that she had always found successful—love of work and belief in what one was doing. In one speech she described Saint Paul as the greatest salesman of the Old or New Testament, for "he went down to Athens where they already had 28 different kinds of religion and sold them another kind." According to Helen, all great merchandisers succeeded because they believed completely in what they were selling: "When we love our work and we believe in our line, we have found something that cannot be taken away from us."

If the Gibson salesmen had any doubts about Helen Steiner Rice and her speechifying, their reservations were tempered by the knowledge that Helen practiced what she preached. She told them about what had guided her through the wilderness of her own life. Her own personal Ten Commandments emphasized optimism:

1. THOU SHALT BE HAPPY
2. THOU SHALT USE THY TALENTS TO MAKE OTHERS GLAD
3. THOU SHALT RISE ABOVE DEFEAT AND TROUBLE
4. THOU SHALT LOOK UPON EACH DAY AS A NEW DAY

5. THOU SHALT ALWAYS DO THY BEST AND LEAVE THE REST TO GOD
6. THOU SHALT NOT WASTE THY TIME AND ENERGY IN USELESS WORRY
7. THOU SHALT LOOK ONLY ON THE BRIGHT SIDE OF LIFE
8. THOU SHALT NOT BE AFRAID OF TOMORROW
9. THOU SHALT HAVE A KIND WORD AND A KIND DEED FOR EVERYONE
10. THOU SHALT SAY EVERY MORNING—I AM A CHILD OF GOD AND NOTHING CAN HURT ME

Since those "commandments" governed her personal outlook, it is not surprising that Helen made friends easily, sustained long relationships characterized by loyalty and trust, and eventually triumphed in the work God had prescribed for her in Cincinnati. The Gibson Art motto, "This is Your Company," succinctly described both what her Gibson "family" meant to Helen and what she viewed as the ideal attitude in the workplace. Never shy about expressing herself, Helen put her thoughts on the matter into verse:

> *This is more than a way to earn your pay . . .*
> *More than a place to report each day . . .*
> *It's part of your life, and the hours spent here*
> *Comprise a big share of your living each year . . .*
> *And that is the reason you never should feel*
> *That you're "JUST A NUMBER or A COG in a*
> *   WHEEL" . . .*
> *For everyone working in this plant with you,*
> *Regardless of what kind of work that they do,*
> *Each day is playing an important, real part*
> *In the present and future of the WHOLE*
> *   GIBSON ART . . .*

Helen
Steiner Rice
Ambassador
of Sunshine

We are "PART of a TEAM" and "A CIRCLE of
  FRIENDS"
Reaching beyond where our own duty ends . . .
Not standing "alone" but as "part of a whole" . . .
Striving together for one common goal . . .
For what man can boast that he won on his own
Or truthfully say "I did this alone" . . .
For everyone holding a job great or small
Contributes a part to the future of all. . . .

The individual friendships Helen established in her first years at Gibson were remarkable for their longevity. As far as she was concerned, loyalty was one of the most important virtues. When she committed herself to a person or a cause, nothing could sway her from the chosen course. Sam Heed, for instance, remained, throughout his life, one of Helen's heroes. He was not simply a man who had been her friend; to Helen, Sam was "a champion of women in business" and an advocate of women's advancement.

Similarly, Bill Dresmann and Helen became lifelong friends. They met soon after she arrived at Gibson. Asked to attend his wedding in October 1935, she treasured the invitation and never forgot the date or the ceremony. In fact, Helen commemorated the event with original anniversary poems and letters to Bill and his wife Irma for the next forty-five years.

Another Gibson friend, George Proud, often picked Helen up at her hotel on Sunday and took her to spend the day with his family. She was so close to the Prouds that when their son was injured in an accident, she gave him shares of stock to cheer him along to recovery.

Adelaide Kerr was a colleague and close friend who spent fifty years at the Gibson Art Company, part of that time as Sam Heed's assistant. When Adelaide retired, Helen wrote a moving, personal tribute to her. Helen's regard was most evident, however, in her gift to Adelaide of a gold coin that had special significance:

> You see, when we were married, Franklin had the very wonderful idea of commemorating the ANNIVERSARY of our MARRIAGE each month with a GOLD COIN. He never had a chance to fulfill this "GOLDEN DREAM." But I kept the COINS he had given me, and, on RARE and SPECIAL OCCASIONS, I have given one of the COINS as a "HEART GIFT."
> . . . So may this little souvenir be a constant reminder, dear, that "YOU ARE WORTH YOUR WEIGHT IN GOLD. . . ."

Helen's assistant in the editorial department, Helen Reid Chase, was especially dear to her. They had an extraordinary relationship, perhaps best seen in nicknames. To Helen, her friend and colleague was "Chasey," and to Chasey, Helen soon became "Rice-Flakes." From the company's point of view, it was a blessing that the two got along so well, for during the 1930s they were responsible for annually matching nearly 25,000 greeting card verses to artistic designs. Helen kept in touch with Chasey long after Chasey moved to the West Coast. Helen did everything she could to encourage and sustain her friend through Chasey's final illness more than forty years after they first met.

Helen had many ways of expressing her love for those she befriended. Some received gifts, others advice and the assurance that she could be counted on no matter what happened. But Helen Steiner Rice was a poet at heart, so her friends were most often the recipients of original verses written to honor them or to commemorate important events. Hal Chadwick, for instance, was a freelance writer who sold some of his work to Gibson. Helen admired his ability and found him a like-minded artist. Although they never met, they developed a mutually rewarding relationship. Hal and his wife, Ruth, kept up a long distance correspondence with Helen—both by letters and phone calls—that spanned decades. When their daughter, Brandy, was born, Helen was chosen to be godmother. The breadth and depth of Helen's affection for the Chadwicks is clear in this personal verse she kept in her diary:

> Sometimes the job of editor
> Seems cold . . . like . . . Winter's Snow . . .
> But along comes folks like "Chadwicks"
> And a cozy little glow
> Is kindled unexpectedly
> We don't know WHEN or WHERE . . .
> We only know we feel the glow
> And are warmed because it's there.

Helen's diary also bears evidence that she began to experiment with spiritual poetry during her earliest years at Gibson. The poem "Sleepy Hollow," written in 1932, touched on one of Helen's favorite themes—how the communion of true friendship was a reflection of God in the world:

> And, in this tranquil rendezvous
> Where peace and beauty blend,
> There is a sweet communion
> In the meeting of a friend;
> For, in this shining solitude,
> False values slip away,
> And only truth and beauty
> Seem planted there to stay.
> The weary one finds comfort,
> The struggling soul finds peace,
> The hungry one finds banquets,
> The bitter one release.

I think this sanctuary
Must be the kind of place
Where very unsuspectingly
We meet God face to face. . . .

When Ethel Brainerd, the editor of the Gibson card lines, died
suddenly, Helen was immediately offered Mrs. Brainerd's job, and
she accepted without a second thought. Helen had long admired
Ethel's writing style—she had even copied several of Ethel's poems
into her diary—but by this time Helen was developing a style and
poetic tradition of her own, one which was rooted in her childhood. By assuming the job of editor at Gibson and accepting its
challenges, Helen embarked on an adventure that gave her creativity many new outlets. One of her earliest published verses, written
for the *Gibson Motto* line in 1934, became an illustrated plaque.
She entitled it "The Golden Chain of Friendship":

*Helen began
work at
Gibson in
1931 as a
trouble-
shooter, but
soon became
editor of
Gibson cards.*

Helen
Steiner Rice
*Ambassador
of Sunshine*

FRIENDSHIP is a golden chain,
The links are friends so dear
Growing just a bit more lovely
With every passing year;
It's clasped together firmly
With a love that's deep and true
And it's rich with happy memories
And glad recollections too;
Time can't destroy its beauty
For, as long as memory lives,
Years can't erase the pleasure
That the joy of friendship gives.

Poignant and sensitive though her style may have been, it was troubling to many executives in a business that was generally resistant to change. Helen Steiner Rice was a pioneer, but the greeting card industry was not yet ready to accept the leadership that would ultimately make her famous. Consequently, throughout the 1930s, Helen found herself constrained to writing verses that tended to be humorous or clever. Some of her cards even became best-sellers, like this one for the 1936 Christmas line:

MERRY CHRISTMAS TO A GOOD EGG!
How do you like your GREETINGS?
Some like 'em FRESH!
Some like a RAW ONE!
Some want 'em WELL DONE!
Some CRAVE them HARD-BOILED!
But MERRY CHRISTMAS
Without any fuss—
Is all that is needed
Between GOOD EGGS like us!

Feature stories on Helen's jingles, or on her assessment of trends in what was fashionable in Christmas cards, appeared routinely in the Cincinnati newspapers. At one point, United Press International carried a Massachusetts woman's claim to be "America's most prolific Christmas card verse writer"; the East Coast poet insisted that she had authored 100,000 verses over twenty-four years. When reporters confronted Helen with the claim, she sneered at the assertion and retorted: "I've been in the business six years and I've written 500,000 greeting card verses. That's a conservative estimate." She may have been exaggerating somewhat, for to do so Helen would need to have written nearly 320 verses every working day.

Helen was an eccentric person in many ways, but it was never clearer than in her disdain of salary. She considered the camaraderie and nurturing she felt during those first years at Gibson to be her real compensation. She quickly came to love her coworkers, as well as the company itself. Consequently, when she was offered a job in New York to head the creative department of a recently formed advertising firm, Helen politely rejected the proposal. By then, she was so committed to Gibson and her colleagues that she found it easy to decline, noting that:

> . . . your offer would mean moving East and severing many connections which are most pleasant to me. . . . In fact, I have been willing to accept a lower salary just because I felt that I was repaid in other ways—through congenial associations and pleasant surroundings. . . .

No one was more aware of the many facets of Helen's personality, especially her boundless enthusiasm, natural ability, and capacity for loyalty and friendship, than Willis D. Gradison. A successful financier, public servant, and member of Gibson Art's board of directors, Mr. Gradison recognized Helen's qualities from the moment she arrived in Cincinnati. A shrewd judge of talent, he

In 1935, Helen Steiner Rice was well known in Cincinnati political circles as speechwriter and speechmaker for Republican Willis D. Gradison, Sr.

liked her style and knew that she would be good for the company. Like Helen, Gradison had lost his father while still a teenager and went to work to support his mother. He first took a job as a board marker for W. E. Hutton while he attended night school at the University of Cincinnati. Then, in 1925, after ten years with Hutton, he formed a stockbrokerage firm, Gibson and Gradison, with his friend Robert Gibson. Five years later, Mr. Gibson left the partnership; but Gradison, undaunted by the fact that America was sinking into the Great Depression, opened his own firm, W. D. Gradison and Company.

Willis Gradison gave as much of his energy, time, and financial expertise to the betterment of his community as he did to his busi-

Helen poured her energy and enthusiasm into the campaigns of Councilman Willis D. Gradison, Sr. in the 1930s.

Helen
Steiner Rice
*Ambassador
of Sunshine*

ness affairs. Because of those civic virtues, Helen saw in him the same dedication to service that had been the driving force in her own life. In 1933, while Willis was an inexperienced Ohio state legislator, he was elected to a two-year term on Cincinnati's city council. During the next seven campaigns, Helen served as his speechwriter because she believed so deeply in what he wanted to accomplish. Doing everything she could to ensure his re-election, Helen played a significant role in the political campaigns of a man best known as "Watchdog of the City Treasury." Helen's public relations efforts nourished the formidable reputation Mr. Gradison acquired for keeping the city fiscally sound during the turbulent 1930s and 1940s.

Once committed to his advancement, Helen poured her inexhaustible talent and energy into Gradison's campaigning efforts. Along with raising money and contributing out of her own pocket,

Helen devoted herself to speechmaking, designing campaign literature, and writing catchy slogans that would persuade Cincinnatians to vote for him.

She summarized her unabashed admiration for Willis Gradison in a fund-raising talk she gave at a "political tea."

> He refuses to talk a spectacular campaign and prefers to produce and accomplish and achieve. . . . He does not possess the finesse of a polished politician, and he is lacking in the subtle art of hand-shaking and back-slapping and merry-mixing. In his public appearances he is quiet and retiring. He is not a honey-voiced orator with a persuasive vote pulling appeal. . . . If you believe that head-work is more essential in City Government than mouth-work, prove it by casting your vote for Willis D. Gradison, the man who believes that "little performance accompanies big talk."

In the autumn of 1939, Gradison was injured in a nearly fatal auto crash, but Helen, loyal as ever, campaigned successfully for his re-election while he recuperated. When he decided to leave Cincinnati's city council after fourteen years of service, she even wrote his speech declining the nomination for an eighth term. His guiding principle—that "the greatest gift in life is giving to others"—perfectly mirrored Helen's sentiments. It is no wonder they had such a long and mutually beneficial relationship.

The Gradison campaigns were only a few of the many political outlets Helen used to express her fervent Republican sentiments. One of the qualities that had attracted her to Franklin Rice, for example, had been his commitment to the political optimism of Herbert Hoover, something that comforted Franklin throughout the days of the Great Depression. Helen shared and sustained that belief in the principles of the Grand Old Party. She characterized Franklin Roosevelt as "cocky," and believed that his welfare programs would bring ruin to the national budget. Indeed, she did everything in her power to oppose Roosevelt's "New Deal."

When Willis Gradison chaired the Cincinnati area's Landon-Knox Committee during the 1936 presidential race, Helen worked hard for Roosevelt's defeat. Undaunted by the Democrats' landslide victory, she scorned it with a verse in which she resigned herself to eating "FDR stew" for the next four years:

. . . So we might as well acquire
A DEMOCRATIC TASTE
And we might as well get used to
THIS DEMOCRATIC WASTE
Because there lies ahead of us
FOUR LONG, EXCITING YEARS
Without much chance or prospect
Of anything that CHEERS,
But there's no use in FUSSING
For the only way to WIN
Is to make the CULPRITS SORRY
That they VOTED THAT GUY IN—
And when I hear NEW DEALERS
Complaining of their lot—
I'll say with SATISFACTION
Well, YOU ASKED for WHAT YOU
GOT!

Willis Gradison naturally shared Helen's political beliefs as much as he appreciated her sense of humor, but the ties that bound them most closely were their faith in God and their belief that optimism would conquer all. He expressed his appreciation of Helen's character best when he wrote a beautiful tribute to her, occasioned by his observance of Yom Kippur, "a day that people devote in prayer and in evaluating their souls and hearts and minds, and also in supplication of forgiveness of sins."

Helen
Steiner Rice
Ambassador
of Sunshine

Through adversity and heartbreaks and seemingly insurmountable sorrows your faith shines like a beacon at night, your courage is invincible and your holy spirit is contagious. You are God's emissary to a sad world. You are His example for all of [us] to follow. And when we pray we see you before us and ask that we too may be as you. I know God blesses you—may He ever do so.

Helen did not only support Willis and Republicanism; she embraced the entire Gradison family. During those first years after Franklin's death, they provided her with a much-needed sense of belonging and helped establish her roots in Cincinnati. By 1936 Helen was so completely integrated into the Gradison family that she joined Willis, his wife Dorothy, and his mother on a Canadian cruise aboard the steamer *Franconia*.

The infamous 1937 Ohio River flood, which devastated Cincinnati, drew Helen even closer to the Gradisons. As the waters rose to record levels, tap water was declared unsafe for drinking, all water was rationed, and electrical service was severely disrupted. Downtown businesses were closed and emergency assistance meant the difference between life and death. Worried about his family, Willis Gradison sent his wife and children to stay with Dorothy's parents in St. Louis while he helped coordinate the relief effort from City Hall. During her absence, Dorothy suggested to Helen that she might join Willis' mother at the family home in Paddock Hills, where she could at least get hot meals and safe drinking water.

With Gibson Art closed Helen had nothing to occupy her time, so she pitched in on the relief work. Serving as liaison between City Hall and the local radio stations, she wrote news releases urging citizens to get injections if they had risked disease by drinking unpurified water. Furthermore, she assumed responsibility for providing regular updates on the grim situation that had closed Cincinnati's business district.

Throughout the crisis, Helen never failed to write every day to Dorothy Gradison. She confided to Dorothy in St. Louis, "Mother

*Dorothy
Gradison
(left) and
Helen relaxed
together on
the deck of
the Franconia
during a
1936 cruise
to Canada.*

Helen
Steiner Rice
*Ambassador
of Sunshine*

is fine physically and has every reason to be happy and cheerful—
NO ONE has NEGLECTED her this week—but she still is far
from being a little sunbeam." While Willis Gradison spearheaded
the relief effort, Helen spent what little free time she had trying to
soothe his fretful mother.

One of Helen's biggest frustrations, she told Dorothy, came
when she returned to the Gibson Art Company at Fourth and
Plum after the city reopened the downtown business district. She
wrote:

And what an AFTERNOON??? I came back to my office and my dear what I found here is worse than the CITY HALL. I am all UPSET and CONFUSED and downright "mad." 300 girls working here with no toilets working at all and they just have to SUFFER and FORGET about the URGE if they can. Then too, no one was paid for time missed during the flood and it is surely an unhappy picture. Why can't employers be more kind and more considerate of those poor unfortunates. Well, that is LIFE.

Ever sensitive to people's needs, no matter what their status, Helen was just as concerned about the welfare of the maids at the Gibson Hotel as she was about the plight of the city's upper crust. To ease the strain on the hotel's support staff, she ran her own little relief service, dispensing cookies, fruit, and juice to them every morning. She explained her actions to Dorothy, writing:

> They don't get the proper food and they are mostly all feeling sick and have colds. You surely see a lot of tragic things since the waters are receding. Homeless people with everything gone and not an idea in the world as to where to start or what to do. And then companys like mine docking them for the time they lost during the flood when the city ordered them to stay home and they could NOT WORK.

In a rare expression of vanity, Helen also confided to Dorothy her distress at not being able to wash her hair: "I could FRY DOUGHNUTS in it—it is so greasy." A few days later, she was nearly frantic for a shampoo, but the doctor's office advised that chemicals required to purify the water mains were so strong that using tap water could "turn a blond into a brunette, make her scalp sore, or cause her hair to fall out!" Helen decided to live with the discomfort a while longer. As the dangers and irritations caused by the flood eased and the waters receded, Helen's mood improved. She turned to verse to give Dottie Gradison a final update:

Nothing much to write about
Nothing much to say—
Nothing much to tell you
It's just another day—
The flood is mostly over
The DISASTER is no more
And CINCINNATI moves along
Much as it did before. . . .

The reason Helen Steiner Rice had so many friendships of such duration was that she never failed to sustain those close to her when they needed a kind word or understanding audience. Equally as important, she never let conflict destroy her relationships. Whenever problems arose, Helen was always quick to resolve them before they could do serious harm. Once, when a misunderstanding occurred between Helen and Dottie, Helen sent her friend a copy of a favorite poem, "Not Understood," by Thomas Bracken. It read in part:

Not Understood, we make so much of trifles;
The thoughtless sentence or the fancied slight
Hast oft destroyed a friendship years in making
And on our souls there falls a chilling blight—
   NOT UNDERSTOOD. . . .
O God, if men could see a little clearer
Or judge less harshly when they cannot see
O God, if men would draw a little nearer
To one another, they'd be nearer then to Thee—
   AND UNDERSTOOD.

Helen
Steiner Rice
Ambassador
of Sunshine

When Dorothy Gradison died in 1971, an inventory of her belongings revealed that copy of Thomas Bracken's poem.

To the Gradison children, Willis, Jr. and Joan, Helen was known as "Aunt Helen." She eagerly assumed the task of looking after them while their parents were away, and wrote detailed reports to Dorothy assuring her that all was well at home. Helen referred to Billy as her "best boyfriend," and she carefully followed his progress in school and at summer camp. For years, young Bill Gradison wondered why his Republican parents had luggage with the monogram "F.D.R." stored in the family attic. He finally realized that "Aunt Helen" had given to his father the luggage that once belonged to her deceased husband.

Joan Gradison was Helen's "angel face," someone Helen had tucked into bed more times than she could remember. One of Helen's fondest memories was Joan's loving assurance that Jesus would always look out for "Aunt Helen." She never forgot the child's prediction, which proved true in more ways than one.

Another relationship Helen carefully tended was the one with her brother-in-law, Elwood Rice. Even though she and Elwood had clashed when Franklin courted and married her, she determined to keep in touch with her husband's brother. She visited him often, corresponded regularly, and graciously accepted Elwood's many gifts. A hand-tooled leather album filled with detailed pictures of his New York apartment, along with a large color portrait of himself—to say nothing of a full-scale advertisement promoting Elwood's pet project, the *Rice Leaders of the World*—served notice that Elwood Rice both needed and depended on Helen's loyalty and love.

Helen's regular summer visits to Elwood in New York were usually occasioned by her plans to cruise abroad, for travel was one of her favorite avocations. In August 1938, for instance, Helen made an impulsive decision to join Sam Heed's wife and another friend aboard the *Vulcania* for a trip to the Mediterranean. What she had thought would be a time of relaxation turned out to be more alarming than restful, for at every port-of-call in Italy, Helen came

Helen Steiner
Rice was
"Aunt Helen"
to the
Gradison
children. Bill
(pictured
with Helen in
1936) was
her "best
boyfriend."

Pictured
together in the
1930s, Helen
called Joanie
Gradison her
"angel face."

Helen
Steiner Rice
Ambassador
of Sunshine

Helen visited her brother-in-law, Elwood Rice, in New York before leaving for a trip abroad in 1938.

face to face with nervous soldiers. She soon wished she had stayed home, describing the Mediterranean Sea as "a navy yard afloat with battleships of European nations trying to discover one another's next move."

"That a war is brewing even the most casual observer can see," she told a reporter from the *Cincinnati Post* when she returned home. But, Helen also predicted, "It seems to me it will be some months yet before the general outbreak." In this interview, published on the front page, she made no effort to conceal her disgust with American tourists who were "blithely unaware of the tempest brewing around them. They went to look at the ruins in the Italian cities and took pictures with their Brownie cameras and were utterly unconcerned with the wretched conditions of many of the people."

What Helen saw in Italy and read about Germany disturbed her deeply. It prompted a notation in her diary on August 30, 1938, about the power of love to transcend violence:

> *. . . And in this story of struggle and strife*
> *That's filled with conflict of human life*
> *The truth and beauty of human love*
> *Rise as a spire beyond and above*
> *The ignorant cruelty that reigns today*
> *Where only terror and force hold sway*
> *To prove that real BEAUTY can never die*
> *But lives after men like HITLER pass by.*

A year later, on the eve of the outbreak of World War II, Helen prepared once again to travel abroad. This time it was not to Europe, but rather to the Caribbean aboard the *Normandie*. Helen's mother, more cautious than her eldest daughter, wrote to her, warning Helen to be careful. "Be not to [sic] generous with your trusting spirit or instinct for all is not gold that glitters."

Still, Anna Steiner knew that her daughter's love of travel was more than just a casual distraction.

> But I can't help . . . wonder if it is worth the effort. . . . But be that as it may, if it brings you a measure of happiness then I am so glad you can do the things you like to do for I realize there are longings in everyone's existence which makes us want to go in search of something or somewhere to find what we expect to satisfy our well being.

Later, Helen herself wrote of the quest her mother mentioned, but she couched it in terms of an awareness of "The Great Tomorrow":

> . . . the very impenetrable mystery which enwraps the ever approaching To-Morrow, is the one thing that keeps the fires of hope con-

stantly burning. No matter what our yesterdays have been to-morrow may be different. As long as we have life the fires of hope cannot die out; the flame may burn low but at the thought of a new day the flame which seemed dead, leaps forward and the sparks once more fly upward to spur us on. Even if our today is filled with sadness and defeat—who can foretell what the next day will bring to us.

Before she sailed aboard the *Normandie*, Helen received yet another job offer, this time from an old friend, Jack Hearst. He hoped to persuade her to abandon the greeting card business and accept a radio contract in New York City. As she had done before, Helen declined, preferring to stay with her friends at Gibson Art. The decision was easy. Remaining at Gibson just seemed like the right thing to do.

127

5

*Tempests
and
Transitions*

By 1939, Helen Steiner Rice was widely acknowledged as one of the leading poets in the greeting card business. As an editor (as well as a creative talent), Helen occupied a unique position at Gibson. Her duties not only required that she compose verses and approve those written by other Gibson staffers, she also made selections from work mailed in by freelance writers. On one occasion, Sam Heed asked Helen to evaluate what she recognized as a dubious submission. Her response was emphatic:

. . . I've a hunch Mr. B just had some yokel knock this out and then submitted it for approval to find out if you MIGHTY MONARCHS of "SMOOCH AND MUSH" really KNOW the ANSWERS. IT'S A "TRAP," my dear S.D.H. I smell SABOTAGE!

On another occasion, Helen had to deal with a woman who sold the same verses to a number of major greeting card publishers. Frustrated by the various companies' inability to stop this practice, Helen expressed her annoyance in verse:

She's got the CRUST
Of a TEN-TON CAKE
And all of the TWISTS
Of a RATTLESNAKE

In December 1939, the Cincinnati Post *featured* Helen *holding her personal* Christmas *card.*

"She's dumb," they say
But I think this DAME
Has OUTSMARTED us all
In the greeting card game . . .

Hard on the heels of that experience came the most mysterious freelance writer of all. No one Helen ever encountered behind her editor's desk at Gibson Art was in the same league as O. O. Doone. He, or more likely she—the puzzle remains unsolved—

Tempests
and
Transitions

contacted Helen in early December 1939, claiming to be an engineer who worked for an electronics company in Boston. In retrospect, it is difficult to ignore the fact that Helen's Massachusetts rival of two years earlier lived a few miles south of Doone's alleged hometown of Wakefield; this coincidence leads one to suspect that "O. O. Doone" was an alias. Nevertheless, in her innocence, Helen treated Doone's overtures seriously. According to the evidence he or she presented, O. O. Doone was a multi-talented individual, an "engineer" who also happened to write poetry as a sideline. The quality of verse was such that Helen eagerly urged Doone to submit some verses that could be used on Valentine's Day cards.

When she returned to her office on January 5, 1940, following a long and happy Christmas visit to Lorain, Helen was surprised to find a large cache of Doone's prospective Valentine's Day rhymes on her desk. Helen responded with an enthusiasm tempered only slightly by suspicion:

> . . . I can't help but marvel at the reckless abandon with which you seem to toss 'em off. Such wholesale cleverness makes criticism a bit difficult. Sometimes you write so almighty "perfect" insofar as conforming to greeting card requirements that I am confident that you are an ex-spreader of sunshine and sentiment. You know the INSIDE RACKET too well to be a novice, and yet, how can I dispute the word of so intriguing a STRANGER??? and run the risk of losing your GENIUS???

It mystified Helen, however, that in the midst of a batch of excellent verses, there also appeared some efforts so awkward that she was inclined to think, despite his talent: "That guy's an engineer after all!" Nevertheless, she picked out a group of rhymes that she felt might suit Gibson's needs, commenting that "you probably would never recognize some of the 'Little Doone Darlin's' after Mama Rice washes their faces and combs their hair, for we do

Helen
Steiner Rice
Ambassador
of Sunshine

reserve the right to put braces on the kids' teeth if they need 'em." Gibson bought eight valentine rhymes from Doone for twenty-two dollars.

By the end of January, the eccentric O. O. Doone—who was now signing his letters familiarly "Nick"—promised his exclusive allegiance to Gibson. Helen authorized the purchase of eight more Doone verses, and encouraged the freelancer to submit Mother's Day and Father's Day greetings. By this time, Helen and Doone had struck up a lively correspondence that freely blended the personal with the professional. Doone described a colorful past that included his genealogical roots in New England, a failed marriage, and a sensitive heart yearning for a friend. His words touched all the most sympathetic chords in Helen. Helen was not, however, alone in her attraction to O. O. Doone. The whole editorial staff at Gibson was intrigued and delighted by the mysterious freelance bard, who claimed he "got red around the ears" when he realized that Helen had shared his earlier letters with her colleagues.

Encouraging the growth of their relationship, Helen sent Doone several items that can only be interpreted as evidence of her growing fondness and regard. Some were old newspaper clippings; others included a card on which she had pasted her picture and written some details of her past. She asked innumerable questions, and Doone responded in kind. "You can ask more questions and give fewer answers than any woman I ever wanted to meet," he chided in a letter mailed to the Gibson Hotel on February 2, 1940.

O. O. Doone left no doubt about his eagerness to be friends with Helen, while at the same time expressing concern that he perceived something distrustful or suspicious in her manner. He also pressed Helen for more information about herself in questions that can easily be interpreted as leading her down a path she was all too willing to follow:

Aren't you doing work you like? Aren't you a successful Career Woman. . . ? Do you write as well as edit? Do you work long hours? Is it hard? What do they do for amusement in the gang you belong to? Why do you live in a hotel. . . ?

If O. O. Doone really was the Massachusetts woman who felt such keen competition with Helen Steiner Rice, it is hard to understand how she could be so cruel as to deceive her rival in this perverse way.

Helen soon received several more verses, but their lack of quality startled her. She wrote back on February 6, 1940, wisecracking that by the time the new verses reached her, they were lifeless: "We used the Pulmotor and the PRONE PRESSURE METHOD OF RESUSCITATION—but to no avail. What in the world happened??? Your mind certainly wasn't on your work that night." Rather than rely solely on her own judgment, Helen showed the verses to two other staffers in the department. Both independently verified her assessment. Clearly disappointed, Helen began to worry that this packet of verses confirmed Doone's self-deprecating claim that he was only an occasionally gifted amateur writer. She returned "the little 'Doone derelicts,'" but couldn't keep herself from purchasing one of them to encourage him. As she explained it, "This is one verse I am not buying because it is a HUMDINGER but only to keep the door open and the welcome mat out."

Doone clearly realized that Helen was torn between her personal curiosity about him and her professional reservations about the inconsistent quality of his verses. He even suggested that it might be a good idea for them to meet face-to-face, in March 1940, while he was in Ohio on business. His last letter reached Helen on February 9, however, and in it Doone indicated that he would not be sending any more rhymes after March.

Helen described his final communication as a "scathing indictment" directed at her personally, one that suggested she "had no friendships or contacts based on a solid knowledge of mutual esteem." Worse yet, from Helen's point of view, Doone accused her of being "suspicious of all mankind and bitter and distrustful of people who were sincere in their striving." She understandably judged the assertions as an "uncalled for and unusual reaction" to her last letter to Doone. She was particularly mystified because her communique had included a check from Gibson and a promise of commissions for future work.

Although she was puzzled and distraught, Helen soon collected herself enough to send off an apology for having possibly offended Doone. It was never acknowledged, nor were any of her subsequent letters. Weeks passed, and as they did, Helen's suspicions about the entire encounter steadily grew. Once she reviewed the cashed checks, and discovered that the endorsements were in a much different handwriting than signatures on the letters, she began to get the uneasy feeling that she had been duped. Helen soon found herself determined to answer the question: Who was O. O. Doone?

On March 7, Helen wrote to the postmaster of the Wakefield, Massachusetts, post office asking if mail in Doone's post office box was still being collected. She explained that Gibson Art Company had received no answers to numerous letters. "The recent behavior of this individual strikes us as most unusual in view of the fact that we had accepted him as a contributor to our lines. . . . We are inclined to believe that there is something peculiar about this entire situation. . . ." She also wrote to the Wakefield Savings and Trust Company, the bank where Gibson's checks to Doone had been cashed, and asked for information about the account under the name of O. O. Doone. Specifically, Helen wanted to know if the patron was a man or a woman. "Our canceled checks show a decidedly womanish signature," Helen explained, "but in all correspondence to us an entirely different signature and style of writing has been used."

Helen's growing fear—that she was dealing with someone who, despite considerable charm and sophistication, was not being honest with her—seemed closer to the truth with every initiative she launched. Her professional pride wounded by the deception, matters were only made worse because Helen felt betrayed on a personal level by this engaging stranger. He, or she, had expressed an interest in Helen's life and past heartaches, and sought in several letters to form a friendship with her. The worst, however, was yet to come. Doone's harshest blow fell a week later, when Helen received a letter from a Wakefield bank officer who reported that the O. O. Doone account had been opened by a woman!

No one likes to be played for a fool, but the pain of it sometimes can be eased by understanding the manipulator's motives. No such relief was available to Helen, so she found herself equally furious and embarrassed. In her response to the bank official, Helen confessed that she had been worried about some sort of duplicity from the beginning, but had been disarmed by the heartfelt sentiments of subsequent letters. An innocent victim of someone's sick joke, Helen's agony found expression in the conclusion of her letter to the bank officer: "What motivated her to carry this deception to such lengths we can not yet deduce. The whole thing makes me feel a bit 'slimy' and I regret that I was so unfortunate as to have ever contacted her and brought her work to the attention of our firm."

In her final letter to O. O. Doone, mailed to the Wakefield post office box address, Helen unleashed her indignation. Expressing her anger in no uncertain terms, she condemned Doone's cunning and demanded the return of her letters and pictures:

There are no words in the English language to express the revulsion, repugnance, and utter contempt that I feel for you. Never in my wide and varied experiences have I contacted a human being so despicable and so devoid of decency and principle. . . . In all its sordiddness, it is a bit sad to think that anyone could so defile and debase a God given talent for beautiful writing.

Helen persisted in torturing herself about the O. O. Doone episode long after it was over. She found it hard to believe that the letters she had received had been written by a woman. Helen tried, without success, to unearth more information, charitably wondering if she had been dealing with a "poor, tortured, warped soul," or, in her darker moments, if Doone should be considered a "person that is dangerous." A few months later, she saw some verses in a competitor's line. The style reminded her of Doone's work, so she inquired about them, but nothing ever came of her investigations. The mystery of O. O. Doone remained unsolved, and Helen found what little comfort she could in a verse that commemorated the writer who had captured the fancy of Gibson's editorial department:

> *I've TELEPHONED and*
> *TELEGRAPHED,*
> *I've WEPT and WORRIED and*
> *LAUGHED,*
> *I've BEGGED and COAXED and even*
> *PLEADED,*
> *I've "GIVEN IN" and I've CONCEDED,*
> *I tried to be SERIOUS—I tried to be*
> *FUNNY—*
> *I was willing to settle for LOVE or for*
> *MONEY—*
> *I tried hard to please you and be a GOOD*
> *SPORT—*
> *I GAMBLED MY ALL and YOU SOLD*
> *me SHORT . . .*

And I won't go so far as to insist you're a
     RAT
But this proves you're a HEEL and a FLAT
     one at THAT.

The O. O. Doone story may have ended in the spring of 1940, but perhaps not. In June 1952, Helen received a strange letter from someone claiming to be a mining engineer whose company was working out of New Philadelphia, Ohio. The writer expressed a hope to meet Helen and have dinner with her in Cincinnati on July 15, before traveling northwestward on business. The letter was signed "Dune," rather than Doone, but written in the post-script was, "I still love you very much." Was this the mysterious freelancer or not? Evidently, Helen was also puzzled by the offer. Next to the postscript, she drew a question mark in red ink.

Even before O. O. Doone dropped from sight, Helen had more work to do at Gibson Art than she had hours in the day to complete it. Fueled by an economic escape from the Great Depression and a steadily rising taste for sentimentality, the greeting card industry enjoyed an unanticipated boom early in the 1940s. The outbreak of World War II in Europe stimulated nationalism at home and created a new set of market demands for Helen to satisfy. Patriotism and "the American way" proved to be the most popular subjects for birthday and anniversary cards. Helen's 1940 birthday card line, for instance, included a dozen cards with patriotic themes. Her personal favorite was one that featured America's symbol of freedom and justice, the Statue of Liberty. The card sent a vital message that was not lost on the thousands who purchased it: "You're getting a real birthday wish from me. May you always live in the land of the free." This card, and others like it, were printed in red, white, and blue.

Meanwhile, Helen's reputation as a versifier of rare talent grew steadily. Greeting cards had become big business, and Helen

Steiner Rice was right in the vanguard. The best testimony to her influence came from Phil Stack, the editor of a Dayton, Ohio, card company. He contacted her in August 1941, with what he called "a plea for help":

> Do you know by any chance, some young thing or some young man, simply dazzling in the realm of verse; someone who dashes off 'the wittiest things' at a moment's notice and yet can turn and do a 'hearts and flowers' job that will have the customers wringing salt tears out of their hankys. This is a mild way of saying that I could use a young assistant who would be a combination James Whitcomb Riley and J. P. McAvoy. I know that such a party would be gobbled up immediately by any greeting card concern, but maybe this gal or guy has a sister or brother at home.

Helen's response indicated she, too, felt Stack's pressing need for more creative writers:

> Goodness—gracious—mercy me! Why, if I should ever get an inkling, glimpse, or slight indication that there existed a human hunk of horseflesh in the world who measured up to just 50% of the STACK SPECIFICATIONS as outlined in your letter of August 5th, I'd track them down with the unflinching bloodhound technique of a Nazi Gestapo. . . .
>
> I am confronted with the same problem you are. I work ten times as hard as I desire, because of necessity. Like yourself, I can't find anyone with the imagination of a flea to help. . . .

Out of their mutual search for the ideal versifier, Helen and Phil Stack soon developed a rewarding professional relationship. Stack, too, was highly regarded as a leader in the field of greeting card verse. He was better known, however, under his pseudonym, "Don Wahn," as the author for more than two decades of heartbreaking verses in Walter Winchell's syndicated newspaper column. After a few years working for the Stanley Company, Stack left and joined Gibson Art in its New York office. A brilliant, creative wordsmith, Stack was a genius whose life was tragically flawed. A long-time sufferer from bouts of deep melancholy, Stack's life was compounded by two catastrophes. In 1941, his toddler son died of a rare kidney disease, and two years later his wife died in child-birth. By then, however, Phil Stack had established a solid link with Helen, so on both occasions her words of comfort helped sustain him. More than anything else, Helen's willingness to share her sense of devastation and grief with him in a comparable situa-tion—after Franklin's death—helped Phil Stack feel as though someone really understood. Despite his sense of desolation, he paid tribute to Helen in a note:

> We have shared an experience that can only bring two minds and hearts closer. Your generous offer to help me is sincerely appreci-ated and you know I will call on you if the weight cannot be sus-tained by me. . . .

A few years later, Stack's second marriage foundered, and even-tually he had to enter a sanitarium following a nervous breakdown. Helen felt his pain keenly, and she did everything humanly possible to comfort and encourage him. He labored to understand how some people grew bitter about failure in life while others were motivated by it, using failure's negative power "as a steppingstone to success." He wrote to Helen in June 1947:

> You speak of your last fifteen years. . . . I marvel at the job you have done . . . but as you say you were true to yourself . . . my trouble is that I find no self to be true to . . . I look inside and there's noth-ing there. . . . I seem to have some facility for turning out verse and that about winds me up as a person . . . but my emotions seem syn-thetic and I don't know any of the answers. Maybe none of us do.

Helen functioned as a moderator of Stack's fierce interior strug-gle. He confided to her:

If I had to be born again I'd like to be one of those guys with a good callous hide who can drink, dance and be merry. . . . I seem to have (and again I suppose it is like us all) a spiritual and sensual side pulling against one another all my life . . . a touch of Bohemian plus a good old New England conscience . . . what a combination. Somehow there must be a way to get a plan of life. . . .

Helen tried unsuccessfully to help Phil Stack find the "plan of life" he was seeking. In March 1948, Stack went to the Gibson Art studio at 35th Street and Madison Avenue in New York and ended his life by plummeting from a twelfth-floor window to the street below.

Helen felt the loss of Phil Stack acutely. Stack's sister, Florence McHarg, deeply appreciated Helen's expressions of comfort, and wrote to her:

You and he certainly understood each other very well—he was lucky to have a wonderful person like you to turn to. He spoke of you very very often. . . . I thank you again from my heart for all these lovely words you sent me— you are so talented—and you use that God-given talent to help us [who are] less fortunate.

The entry of the United States into World War II presented Helen with a dilemma that again tested her sensitivity. Gibson Art anticipated a boom in greeting card sales as those at home attempted to cheer and communicate with the millions of men and women in the armed forces. Helen reflected thoughtfully on the best way to meet this need for a new series of cards. "I didn't know whether to make them sentimental or funny," Helen explained at one point when interviewed by a newspaper reporter. "There were those who told us they should be funny to cheer the boys up, but reports from camp indicate that the boys seem to want the sentimental kind." She was torn between wanting to do the right thing for those in the armed forces and help Gibson maintain its place as a leader in the market.

In creating her personal Christmas card in 1942, however, Helen elected to follow her heart. She chose the inspiring themes of peace, fellowship, and freedom:

> *May Christmas this year, amid chaos,*
> *cruelty and conflict, be a blessed*
> *instrument through which we can find*
> *comfort and courage and cheer in the*
> *communion of our hearts.*
> *May we discover, this Christmas, the*
> *sustaining powers of a strong faith*
> *and the abiding values of courage,*
> *heroism, honor, fellowship and freedom.*
> *May our MATERIAL GIFTS be LESS*
> *And our SPIRITUAL GIFTS GREATER.*
> *"Peace on Earth, Good Will to Men" is*
> *not an empty dream. It is the MIRACLE*
> *of Christmas—and such MIRACLES are*
> *made of FAITH and BRAVE HEARTS.*
> *May God bless America and you,*
> *and may the New Year find us all not only*
> *SAFE but FREE.*

Helen's thoughtful choice of verses for her first wartime card reflected changes that had occurred in her. Some of these were the natural result of a wisdom that only comes with maturation; others were precipitated by tragedy and disappointment. As her spirituality deepened, Helen's vision of humankind broadened, and her sense of humor, always keen, took on a new dimension. Experience was undoubtedly Helen's chief teacher, but her love of reading also accounted for a constantly expanding and important source of insight.

Helen's friends and coworkers knew her as an avid reader—how else would she have been able to come up with such an inexhaustible store of literary allusions and references—but few knew how hard she worked at it. Just as she consumed books by the score, Helen also kept extensive files of newspaper clippings and innumerable excerpts carefully copied from her best-loved literary works. Ahead of her time, she kept an open mind, happy to distill wisdom from any source that presented itself. Her reference files are as remarkable for their range as they are for sheer numbers, including such diverse materials as quotes from the Chinese philosophers Lao Tze and Confucius, as well as observations from the newspaper columns of Bishop Fulton Sheen. Certain themes—love, tolerance, wisdom, forgiveness, appreciating life, and keeping a cheerful outlook—dominated her compilation of materials as Helen fed her mind on the insights she gleaned from others. Intellectually austere writers like Ayn Rand intrigued her, but she just as eagerly devoured romance novels, popular psychology, unsophisticated poetry, and nearly everything in *Reader's Digest*. At the same time, Helen was equally comfortable with the writings of classical authors.

With her lively mind, vivacious manner, and seemingly ageless good looks, Helen never failed to attract attention. Joseph Marshall was a teenager in the choir at Wesley Chapel in Cincinnati when he first saw Helen Steiner Rice in the 1940s. He recalled that Helen's arrival at church was always an event, for everyone was invariably impressed, happy to "behold her beautiful impeccable attire and sincere pretty smile. Everything about Mrs. Rice was poetic."

As she entered her forties, Helen was less certain of her physical appeal. A *Cincinnati Enquirer* photographer snapped a candid picture of her in the Gibson Hotel flower shop in August 1943, and asked for permission to publish it. Her hesitation, which she

Helen worried that this candid snapshot, featured in the Cincinnati Enquirer in August 1943, might reveal her "middle-aged flaws."

144

expressed in verse, reveals the self-doubt she began to experience when she felt her girlish sparkle had begun to fade:

> *My eyes are getting "baggy"*
> *My hair is getting "thin"*
> *And a picture isn't something*
> *That I welcome with a grin . . .*
> *For when your sex appeal ain't sizzling*
> *And your tummy's full of gas*
> *And your "uppers and your lowers"*
> *Spend their evenings in a glass . . .*
> *Then a PICTURE in the PAPER*
> *Is risky stuff allright*

Helen
Steiner Rice
*Ambassador
of Sunshine*

And a gal can't be too careful
When she plays with dynamite.

Helen's objections to publishing the photo were met with equally good spirit and cleverness by the *Enquirer's* advertising manager, Robert O'Dowd. He joined in the repartee with a verse of his own, albeit one that encouraged her to sign the release form.

"Charms" that you have been parading
All about your beauty "Fading"
Leave me cold.
For I've heard a different story,
That your eyes are "pools of glory"
Hair of "gold."
If perchance it gives you trouble
That your chin is really "double"
Don't you dare!!!!
Teeth like "yours" are pearls, appealing
True or false, they have me reeling
In despair.
Now, if you'll desist your "slighting"
Take your pen and start to writing
T'will be fine.
On your name I am depending
All our troubles will be ending
When you sign. . . .

Amused by O'Dowd's clever response, Helen finally elected to sign the release. She could not, however, return it to the *Enquirer's* advertising manager without a final parting shot—one that perhaps revealed more than she intended—in rhyme:

Being FEMALE I am FLATTERED
Even though my "HULK" is battered
And you really must admit it is a "HULK"!
I have seen my SAGGING TORSO
And your camera made it MORE SO
For it magnified my ever BULGING
*   BULK....*
I look like a night club bouncer
Or a wrestling match announcer....
You have stripped me of all feminine
*   allure????*
I know well I'm not a GRABLE
No one fights to buy me sable
But I still keep looking for L'AMOUR....

A few days later the picture about which so many stanzas had been exchanged appeared in the Sunday edition of the *Cincinnati Enquirer*.

As World War II dragged on, Helen was personally affected by the fate of her coworkers at Gibson who served their country. To do her part, she agreed to become editor of the *Gibsonews*, a company effort designed to cheer Gibson employees in the service. In *Gibsonews*, Helen Steiner Rice touched the lives of G.I.'s with a unique blend of humor, current events, sentimentality, and social commentary:

We suppose you are all anxious to know "WHAT'S COOKIN'" back here in Cincy! Candidly, the answer is . . . "WE ARE!" . . . The gals all are bemoaning the fact that their "RAYON HOSE" are falling like G.I. TENTS around their shapely ankles . . . but we guess that into every woman's life a little "RAY-ON must FALL" . . . only we wish it was the right kind of "RAIN" for we are having

Helen
Steiner Rice
*Ambassador
of Sunshine*

An effervescent Helen spread good cheer during World War II by editing the Gibsonews, which was sent abroad to Gibson employees in the armed services.

a drought along with this HEAT MENACE, and our national anthem has become "HOW DRY WE ARE!"

Helen put a lot of effort into Gibson's newsletters. By Christmas 1944, when Hitler's last ditch offensive in the West—the Battle of the Bulge—raged, she produced an elaborate rhymed edition. Among other things, it mentioned by name every Gibson employee engaged in the war effort and included how and where they were serving their country.

In the midst of her efforts to cheer and console others, Helen suffered a great personal loss. Her mother died suddenly of a heart attack in February 1945. For Helen and Gertrude, their mother's

death proved to be "the darkest hour" of their lives. Ever practical and methodical, Mrs. Steiner had prepared her children for her death as she advanced into her seventies. She made careful arrangements with a Lorain funeral home, and three years earlier had written out her own death notice. She had also discussed her impending "journey into eternity" with her daughters.

So, when Helen was notified of her mother's passing, Anna Steiner's words came back to her. They inspired her to write the poem she originally called "My Mother's Message to Me." Helen realized that the verse, which expressed her private grief, might help others who had suffered a comparable loss. She decided to share the poem, and when it was published by Gibson it became a best-seller as a sympathy card:

The sudden
death of Anna
Steiner in
February
1945 inspired
Helen to write
the poem
"When I Must
Leave You."

149

When I must leave you for a little while
Please do not grieve and shed wild tears
And hug your sorrow to you through the
    years,
But start out bravely with a gallant smile;
And for my sake and in my name
Live on and do all things the same,
Feed not your loneliness on empty days
But fill each waking hour in useful ways,
Reach out your hand in comfort and in cheer
And I in turn will comfort you and hold you
    near,
And never, never be afraid to die
For I am waiting for you in the sky!

Among the numerous messages of consolation that Helen and Gertrude Steiner received when their mother passed away was one which also proved to be a further source of inspiration to Helen. Her friend and traveling companion, Elizabeth Heed, wrote in her brief note of comfort, "And so another fine soul has burst its chrysalis of clay and fared forth upon a new realm of usefulness! May you and your sister gather many lovely lilies of remembrance as you go thru Memory's garden." Two months later, when President Franklin Roosevelt died, the images Mrs. Heed evoked led Helen to reflect again in verse on the theme of eternal life. The *Gibsonews* carried her moving testimonial to the man who had led the nation through one of its greatest crises, its first lines obviously guided by Elizabeth Heed's sentiments:

> *He burst his chrysalis of clay*
> *And fared forth to another realm*
> *Where he can lend his usefulness*
> *To God, at the heavenly helm . . .*
> *. . . We may not have been in agreement*
> *With his politics or his plan*
> *But the world is touched and sobered*
> *At the "GOING HOME" of this man,*
> *And we bow our heads as Americans*
> *And pray that he may be blest*
> *With EVERLASTING VICTORY*
> *And ETERNAL PEACE AND REST.*

The last appearance of *Gibsonews* was in September 1945, six months after the Nazis had been defeated and a few weeks after the first two atomic bombs had forced the Japanese to surrender. The newsletter's final issue featured a poem by Helen advising that the long-sought end of hostilities included a challenge to heal a wounded world and bring it back to life:

> *. . . Keep us grateful, Omnipotent God,*
> *And aware of those sleeping beneath the sod,*
> *Strengthen our bonds one with another*
> *So we may dwell as brother to brother,*
> *Heal the wounds and be with us yet,*
> *Lest we forget! Lest we forget!*

With the conclusion of armed conflict came far-reaching re-adjustments to a peacetime economy. Helen found that life at Gibson Art was a microcosm of the difficult postwar transitions taking place across the country. Soon after the war ended, Helen became aware of the rise of a "new order" at the Gibson Art Company, something she found terribly unsettling because she felt it exalted accounting procedures and ignored the camaraderie essential to a creative enterprise. Feeling "saddened and sobered" by what was happening to "OUR FAMILY at GIBSON," she unwillingly resigned herself to the "JUGGERNAUT" that worshiped balance sheets and ignored the human consequences of layoffs and termi-nations. Although the postwar changes required her to make a superhuman effort to readjust, Helen again demonstrated her steadfast loyalty to Gibson. Her childhood friend, Scoop Dumont—by now a prominent businessman—wrote to her in December 1945, trying to woo her into a job with a national advertising firm that had branches in New York, Cleveland, and Chicago. Somehow, despite her worries about the direction Gibson was taking, Helen resisted Dumont's tempting offer and remained loyal to the organization that had given her a chance when she desperately needed one.

Loyalty did not, however, mean that Helen was silent or blind to the changes occurring around her. In June 1946, she wrote to a friend who had just been fired by Gibson:

> . . . what is happening here is only typical of what is happening everywhere in this mad, crazy, confused world, only I think it hurts so much more when it happens to the thing we have cherished and nurtured and believed in for so many years. But the human soul has fallen into disrepute, and for lack of sustenance it is withering and dying, and for lack of light it is becoming blind. Expansion, greed, possessions and selfishness have usurped the place of peace and contentment.
>
> But business without ETHICS is like a WOMAN without HONOR . . . they are both headed for hell. We are dancing on a volcano, but who can stop the wild tom tom beats of greed in a mad world that is drunk with lust for power. . . .

Faced with disillusionment, Helen wrote a poem to the editor of *Public Service Magazine* indicating how wistfully she looked back on her early years in business:

REMEMBER ME??????????
Of course, you don't
Think hard and long
And still you won't
But I am sure you'll recollect
If you will pause and just reflect
When "LIGHT and POWER"
Was "CURRENT" chatter
And folks were paid
To kinda scatter
A bit of sales talk
Now and then
Among the clubs

And business men—
And one "brave" female
Stumped the state
And stalked before
The small and great
And she became known
Not as Helen Elaine
But a "windy" TORNADO
That hailed from LORAIN;
But oh, what changes time can bring
To EVERYONE and EVERYTHING
But 'tis with pleasure I recall
When no one knew my name at all
And when a little bit of praise
Was equal to a good sized raise
And don't I wish
That once again
I'd find the FUN
That I knew then.

Helen's poignant reflection did not, however, mean that she had retreated before the changes that came after the Second World War. In fact, she adapted just as well to those modifications as she had to the ones that accompanied the Great Depression.

It was Helen's firm belief that life's misfortunes often led to the discovery of goodness hidden in others. She herself was the bearer of a special brand of kindness that brightened the world around her. Once, when a male employee working the night shift at Gibson was assaulted and robbed while walking into town for dinner, Helen decided to offer him protection. She often stayed over until the nine o'clock dinner break, so she made the man promise he would not leave the building until she could escort him into town!

Conversely, when someone unexpectedly cheered Helen she went out of her way to reciprocate. In her expansive generosity she reached out to everyone—sales clerks, waitresses, and elevator operators deserved the same consideration as close friends and colleagues. As a case in point, Helen so warmly acknowledged the service of a saleswoman at Pogue's department store that her thank-you was published in the store's newsletter!

> *. . . And of all the pleasant happenings*
> *I have had along life's way. . . .*
> *I don't recall a nicer one*
> *than what you did today.*
> *For in this selfish, careless world*
> *It's rarely that we find*
> *that anyone is THOUGHTFUL*
> *or takes time to be kind. . . .*
> *And when you called me up today*
> *I felt a little "glow"*
> *and I said, "there is a lady*
> *who I'm mighty glad to know."*
> *It was a little thing to do*
> *and yet it was so NICE. . . .*
> *It will NEVER BE FORGOTTEN*
> *by Helen Steiner Rice.*

If Helen's relationships with casual acquaintances and colleagues were remarkable, her devotion to her sister Gertrude was unparalleled. The Steiner sisters had been close since childhood, and neither the years nor the miles between Lorain and Cincinnati served to separate them. Throughout their lives, they spent every holiday together. They wrote to each other on a daily basis, and in later years also called each other every night. Although Gertrude (known fondly to Helen as "Pedro") was the quieter and less flamboyant of the Steiner daughters, she was certainly Helen's equal in determination. In fact, whenever Helen ran up against "Pedro's" resolve, she knew better than to resist. "I know PEDRO is DYNAMITE to HANDLE, and she surely makes it TOUGH for the OTHER GUY. . . ." Helen once wrote to a mutual friend as she fretted over her sister's illness.

Gertrude's hospitalizations in the late 1940s are good examples of Helen's loving respect for her sister. They also provide insight into Helen's understanding of Gertrude's personality. It took all of Helen's willpower to resist her inclination to race to Gertie's side immediately when she fell ill. In the end, Helen elected to stay in Cincinnati, for she realized that "I would only be there wringing my hands and Pedro is such a STOIC she would rather hide her feelings and her pain. . . ." Instead, Helen waited until Gertrude went home from the hospital, predicting that by the time she reached Lorain she would probably "find Pedro sprinkling the yard or maybe finishing the wall washing. . . . [S]ometime I am going to CLIP HER ORNERY LEETLE WINGS," Helen threatened, but then thanked "Brush" Sage, a friend of the Steiner sisters, for helping Gertrude. Then she noted, "I guess that is what FRIENDSHIP is for . . . we love people for their GOOD POINTS and we love them enough to OVERLOOK their 'IDIOSYNCRASIES. . . .'"

The extent of Helen's worry over her sister's health, however, was never clearer than when Gertrude faced unexpected surgery. Helen admitted that "after a week of suspense and anxiety I felt pretty limp when the pressure and tension was removed. . . . I had galvanized myself into action for the fight and when the fight was over I was ready to crumble up." Despite Helen's concern, Gertrude recovered, and the bond between the Steiner sisters grew stronger through the years.

Tempered by life's continuing challenges and tragedies, Helen Steiner Rice gave liberally of herself to support others. She understood that it was not entirely possible to "lift the load from the other guy's heart," but she tried her best to ease everyone's burden. Sometimes she failed and other times she succeeded.

In June 1948, when Joan Gradison graduated from high school, Helen shared an important piece of her own philosophy:

> What happens to you in the years that lie ahead is not as important as how you take what happens to you. And the real secret of happiness is not in doing what one likes to do, but in liking what one has to do. All real knowledge is gained along the pathway of experience . . . and HOW MUCH YOU "GET" depends on HOW MUCH YOU "GIVE." The way of real growth is not to become more famous and more powerful but to become more human and more tolerant. Gold has no value unless it is reminted into goodness, and a beautiful face without a beautiful soul is but a hollow masque.

6

Everything
Changes

elen never viewed anyone who crossed her path as insignificant; she cherished all she met as equals in God's choir, so no kindness was ever too small to go unnoticed and every offense became an object of forgiveness. For years, she lovingly referred to Ida Ginn, the maid who cleaned her room at the Gibson Hotel, as "Mom," kissing her good-bye as she left for work. Once, when a transient guest observed the parting ritual, he innocently commented to Mrs. Ginn: "It sure is nice that you can have your daughter live so close." Helen felt complimented by the remark.

Similarly, the maintenance supervisor of the Gibson Hotel was a regular recipient of letters from Helen praising his performance, especially after he solved problems and made her life easier. After all, life in a hotel was at best a lonely business, so Helen was grateful for anything—a noisy radiator quieted or a dripping faucet returned to working order—that gave her a sense of belonging, a feeling that someone cared about her. The same imperative operated in behalf of the man who was assigned to hang the drapes in Helen's room, for he earned a special commendation. "YOU ARE WONDERFUL," Helen wrote, and continued: "How tragic it is that in this modern world, we have so little time for TRUE

Visiting
Gertrude
in Lorain in
the 1940s,
Helen
exemplified
the height
of fashion.

BEAUTY. It breaks my heart to see shabby, shoddy methods smother to death the skilled beauty of true artists. I am proud and lucky to have known an artist like you." As might be expected, Helen also sent special holiday greetings to the Gibson Hotel's elevator operator as well as the waitresses, bus boys, chefs, and kitchen crew at a nearby restaurant.

By this time, Helen was well recognized at the Gibson Hotel in downtown Cincinnati. She had lived there for more than a decade when Carl Portune was hired to play the piano and solovox in the hotel's Sidewalk Cafe. Since Helen ate most of her evening meals there, the two artists naturally struck up a friendship. Carl was the product of a musically talented family whose members were profi-

Helen— and her hats— always seemed to attract attention.

cient on a variety of instruments. Most comfortable with keyboards, Portune developed his skills on the organ, piano, and solovox. Before a severe heart attack forced him to curtail his activities, he had performed on radio and had served as conductor of the orchestra at the Strand Theater. His music struck a responsive chord in Helen and her presence seemed to animate his performance.

One of the writers for *Your Host* magazine noticed the symbiosis between Helen Rice and Carl Portune. Christening Helen "The Lady with the Hat," he observed that when Helen entered the Sidewalk Cafe, the music changed, gained "a lilting rhythm," and became more "soulful" under her inspiration. As time passed, Carl Portune and Helen became dear friends. Typically, she wrote

Helen
Steiner Rice
*Ambassador
of Sunshine*

verses that celebrated birthdays, anniversaries, and holidays for Portune's wife, Coletta, as well as for his mother and his aunt. Additionally, Helen was so inspired by her connection with Mr. Portune that she found time to write a tribute to his artistry:

"BRIGHTEN THE CORNER WHERE YOU ARE"

> *is our job while living here . . .*
>> *And you've BRIGHTENED UP THE*
>> *SIDEWALK*
> *and BROUGHT A LOT OF CHEER . . .*
>> *For your MUSIC is the "BRIGHT SPOT"*
> *I enjoy every night*
>> *And it makes up for a lot of things*
> *that are not always right . . .*
>> *I'd like to make this statement*
>> *as a patron and a guest . . .*
>> *Of all the music I have heard,*
> *I like YOUR MUSIC BEST . . .*
>> *I've lived in hotels all my life—*
> *abroad, as well as here . . .*
>> *And you play the kind of music*
> *that is GOOD year after year . . .*
>> *. . . And while you get no "OSCAR"*
> *or ACADEMY AWARD . . .*
>> *Or a "Million Dollar Bonus"*
> *voted to you by "THE BOARD" . . .*
>> *I think perhaps OLD GABRIEL*
> *will stick an "EXTRA STAR"*
>> *In "YOUR CROWN" for having*
>> *BRIGHTENED UP*
>> *THE CORNER WHERE YOU ARE.*

161

It was their mutual admiration that, in 1948, led to the creation of two unique greeting cards featuring lyrics by Helen Steiner Rice and music by Carl Portune. "Hush-A-Bye Honey" was, in Helen's words, "a hauntingly hummable little lullaby." It was also an experiment, for the words and music were included inside a card congratulating parents on the birth of a new baby. Whatever anyone else may have thought, Helen was as proud as a new mother of this joint creative venture, and she was determined to see her offspring achieve success. Energetic to a fault, Helen sent copies of it to women's page editors of newspapers in Lorain and Cincinnati, and her efforts were mentioned in articles carried in the *Lorain Journal* and the *Cincinnati Enquirer*. Helen even wrote to Kate Smith, "America's First Lady of Radio." Since Helen had previously crafted a special birthday tribute for Kate Smith from the greeting card industry, she suggested that Miss Smith was "the ideal lady to sing THIS LULLABY." It had, after all, become so popular that it was being sung in churches throughout Ohio, Kentucky, Indiana, and Pennsylvania on Mother's Day in 1948.

The collaborative effort that gave rise to "Hush-A-Bye Honey" was soon followed by Portune's attempt to put Helen's poem "When I Must Leave You," written on the occasion of Anna Steiner's death, to music. Like the lullaby, this blend of words and music provided the basis for a greeting card that carried a message of condolence and offered "A Song of Sympathy to Soften Your Sorrow." A third collaborative venture in the form of a Christmas song called "Tiny Tim" was performed at holiday parties for children in 1950, but the music was never published.

Since she had made such a commitment to the man she once dubbed "Pianissimo Portune," it is understandable that Helen was both anguished and outraged when the Sheraton Corporation, which had taken over management of the Gibson Hotel, made the decision in 1951 to dismiss Portune. She directed a furious letter-writing campaign aimed at Sheraton officials, personally authoring

Pianist Carl Portune (left), Helen, and Elwood Rice share an evening in the Gibson Hotel's Sidewalk Cafe in 1950.

many of the letters later signed by supporters of her cause. The common theme of the protest was a plea that the company spare him because so many patrons enjoyed Carl's music. By now, Helen had mastered the art of expressing displeasure, and her skills were admirably demonstrated in a letter she wrote to an executive of the Sheraton Corporation:

> Your genius as hotel operators with a flair for fancying up fading hotels is nationally recognized and undisputed . . . but even "WIZARDS" can be "TOO WISE." . . .
>
> A vast number of Cincinnatians, including myself, were unpleasantly shocked and surprised and completely confounded to learn that you are dispensing with the inimitable Dinner Music of Carl Portune. Perhaps we are utterly selfish, but there is a large clique of people who have come to feel that his music washes away the dust of the day. . . .

In the end, Helen's efforts in Carl Portune's behalf—admirable though they were—proved ineffective. Although the campaign to save Portune was a failure, the bond of friendship between the pianist and his champion was strengthened by the experience. Years later, when his health was failing, Carl Portune recalled Helen's support and wrote a touching letter to her. It was as much a tribute to friendship as it was an affirmation of how much she continued to inspire him:

> On this dark and dreary rainy day you are the only person to whom . . . anyone could write a very nice letter 'cause after reading your verses (and I do mean we have read and reread them over and over) no one and I mean no one should let their heart be troubled—in hours of discouragement. God is our encouragement how true that is—so you see little Gutsel [a pet name Carl had given Helen] your verses dig deep into one's soul and give great great comfort. Everything you have written has been of the very best and if you recall I always said "HONEY YOU SURE CAN WRITE (PERIOD)."

Why would Helen Steiner Rice involve herself so aggressively in the fate of someone who had become a friend mostly through the force of circumstance? Loneliness may have had a lot to do with it. Virtually from the moment she moved to Cincinnati, Helen surrounded herself with friends, but her solitary existence in a downtown hotel for much of her life bespeaks an essential isolation. While many of her best friends were men, most of them were married. An attractive woman, she had many opportunities for romance. Over the years she may have contemplated remarriage, but this poem to an unidentified recipient—evidently someone she viewed as a viable candidate for her hand—leaves no doubt about Helen's mixed feelings:

> Sometimes I LIKE YOU
> Sometimes I DON'T
> Sometimes I COULD

Sometimes I WON'T,
SOMETIMES YOU SLAY ME
With your CONCEIT
Sometimes I think
You're kinda "SWEET" . . .
But I guess the fact
That you GET MY GOAT
Is still more reason
For you to gloat . . .
'Cause if you're FOR ME
And I'm for you
In spite of all that
We say or do,
We'll MARRY and live to say
"WHAT LUCK!"
Or REGRET IT FOREVER
Because WE GOT STUCK.

The postscript at the bottom of the page speaks volumes: "P.S. I'm not a RICH WIDOW—I'm a POOR WORKING GAL, So if you're after MONEY—I'm the WRONG NUMBER PAL."

More than one of Helen's confidants believed that while she enjoyed the pleasures of being courted, she had little interest in the mundane details of sustaining a household. Helen left her own summary on the matter of matrimony typed, but undated, at the bottom of a poem about successfully tackling life's troubles. She wrote, "The REGRET OVER WHAT I HAVE MISSED in not re-marrying is swallowed up in THE RELIEF at WHAT I HAVE ESCAPED." At this stage of her life it seems that her profession had won so much of Helen's allegiance that personal feelings had to be relegated to a secondary position.

Gibson Art, which Helen had nicknamed the "house of heart throbs" after the war, celebrated its centennial in 1950, and decorated the marquee over the plant's entrance with a half-ton, three-layered, ornamental mock-up of a birthday cake. Helen was fully

166

involved in the anniversary festivities. Invitations sent to the families and friends of Gibson employees to attend an open house at the Fourth and Plum Street home offices carried a special verse written by Helen. For the plant tours, she penned a separate poem called "The Birth of a Greeting Card." It was a rhymed, step-by-step guide through the processes involved in card-making and included a visit to her editorial department:

> *In the BIRTH of a CARD the FIRST OPERATION*
> *Is, as it should be, "AN ACT of CREATION" . . .*
> *So, on the 4th floor, in the DEPARTMENT of ART,*
> *Some artist gives a CARD its start,*

Helen
Steiner Rice
Ambassador
of Sunshine

A little paint and a clever line
And the artist presents a new design . . .
From there it leaves the scene of art
And goes to get itself "heart"—
For any card without a greeting
Is like a visit without a meeting,
So down to the EDITORIAL it goes
For a sentiment written in rhyme or prose. . . .

The headline of a *Cincinnati Post* article on Gibson's centennial proclaimed: "Sentimental Gibsons: They Haven't Said One Unkind Word in Their 100 Years." The author quoted Helen as saying that her job was unlike any other: "It's a job in which you say only kind things." In a world that had grown increasingly harsh and bitter, the story continued, "Mrs. Rice and Mrs. Chase . . . are every day at their typewriters thinking up new, kindly things to say on greeting cards." Helen confessed to the reporter that she frequently became tearful when writing sentimental verses, and tried her best to live according to the kindly feelings she expressed.

Much to Helen's embarrassment, the newspaper used an old, 1938 photograph of her with the story. In time, the author apologized for the error. He claimed, "When I looked at it in the paper, I said, 'This can't be the same gal. The one I met at Gibson's was so much handsomer.'" In a forgiving mood, Helen responded in good humor: "Your flattery has won you a reprieve . . . all is forgiven. Anyhow, a woman should not condemn a man for making her twelve years younger. . . ." Still, she couldn't resist the opportunity this gaffe presented to do a little "preaching":

But "HANDSOME IS
  AS HANDSOME DOES" . . .

And the fact that I looked
like I used to was . . .
I'll have to admit was a
blow to my pride . . .
But God likes me best when
I'm HANDSOME INSIDE.

Although good cheer and loving sentiments flowed easily from her pen, Helen was keenly aware that the world was undergoing dramatic shifts. She was, for example, appalled when the detonation of an atomic bomb by the Soviet Union prompted the United States to produce a more powerful hydrogen bomb. Shortly thereafter, when war broke out in Korea, Helen lamented to a friend in the service:

> It is about time that we gave our souls a chance to catch up with the things that our hand and brain have accomplished. I think we need to KNOW a little less, and UNDERSTAND a little more. We have the menacing marvel of the Atom Bomb, but it is nothing compared to the soul-stirring miracle of the rose petal and the snowflake.

Man can make an ATOMIC BOMB
With great destructive power
But GOD ALONE knows how to make
A SNOWFLAKE and a FLOWER.

May 1951 be brighter for us all than what the beginning portends.

As she grew more reflective, Helen laid much of the blame for the world's problems on greed, so the eternal human inclination to put too much stock in the power of money captured her creative imagination. "It takes more than the almighty dollar to cement relations between countries and individuals," she remarked to a friend. Later, she expressed the same feelings in rhyme:

The MORE you GIVE, the MORE YOU GET . . .
   nobody can deny . . .
And if anyone disputes this . . .
   just let them go and try . . .
And if this GREEDY WORLD today
   would only start to give . . .
Life everywhere, for everyone
   would be more sweet to live . . .
For happiness is only found
   in bringing it to others . . .
And thinking of the folks next door
   as sisters and as brothers.

Helen's concerns about the state of the world did not, however, lead her to forsake a favorite pastime. To her, travel was a great adventure, and nothing kept her from it. Yet an autumn trip to Europe in 1951 left her feeling depressed, "soul sick," and melancholy about nearly everything around her. To a friend she wrote, "I came home battered, beaten, baffled, bewildered and bogged down, with the weight of the OLD WORLD and its WOES crushing very heavily on my soul and my mind." In a letter to another longtime friend A. L. Friedlander, Helen elaborated:

I realize in my heart that the only people who are having a good time in Europe today are the tourists. It is like dancing and laughing in a tomb, and the only sounds that come back to you are the echoes of your own merriment. It seems almost selfish and callously cruel to go gaily flaunting our wealth and well-being in these war-weary countries. And all the progress that man has made, somehow leaves me cold . . . for he has never learned the simple lesson of living with the man next to him . . . so, in spite of our WORLDLY SUCCESSES, we are still SPIRITUAL FAILURES.

It was not just the crushing burden of defeat she saw during her travels abroad that troubled Helen; it was also the increasing cynicism she confronted every day, even in the sentimental business of selling greeting cards. Her draft of a speech she delivered to a physicians' group offers a revealing insight into her painful appreciation of the new postwar order:

> Maybe your patients say, "Oh Doc, have a heart," when you start to work on them. It's just an expression we use with flippant thoughtlessness but this casual slang expression has a deep underlying meaning that if practiced could revolutionize not only our lives but the whole universe. . . .
>
> I am in the business of what is supposed to HAVE A HEART . . . I've been in it just twenty years, but each day of those twenty years we have cut a little more of the heart out of it . . . because we are ASHAMED to HAVE A HEART . . . afraid to be called a SENTIMENTALIST. . . .
>
> The mind . . . measures everything today . . . we have pushed our minds way out ahead but if WE KNEW LESS and FELT MORE . . . we would all be less restless and unhappy and groping in the darkness for something we will never find with only the coldness of our minds . . . there must be the warmth of the heart . . . to touch the soul with sunshine. . . .

Helen never avoided the challenge of dealing openly with issues others either preferred not to see or declined to address. This admirable trait was never more evident than when she confronted the physical and emotional changes of mid-life. In an era when women's health problems were mentioned in whispers or discreetly ignored, Helen turned her sensitivity and intelligence to this vitally important subject. She began writing, with candor and good humor, about the aging process and woman's universal experience—menopause. In her letters and rhymes to friends, Helen openly explored being a female "at that certain crucial stage,"

170

Helen
Steiner Rice
Ambassador
of Sunshine

Even in the 1950s, Helen argued that greeting cards needed the "warmth of the heart *1/1* to touch the soul with sunshine."

blithely ignoring the unwritten taboo that women should suffer through the "change of life" quietly and alone.

"Meno-PAUSE isn't the PAUSE that REFRESHES . . . I'll take COCA-COLA," she wrote to one couple, cleverly signing herself a "Withered Grain of Rice." To a young friend who asked to see a copy of Helen's 1927 Speaker's Bureau brochure, she responded with a poignant verse:

> *But remember what you read in here . . .*
> *Is only "ANCIENT HISTORY," dear . . .*
> *And while it's true I'm "STILL ALIVE"??*
>   *(questionable)??*
> *I've CHANGED a LOT since "TWENTY-FIVE" . . .*
> *And HOW I'VE CHANGED is so alarming . . .*

Everything

Changes

Instead of someone GAY and CHARMING...
I'm just a gal with lots of "middle age flaws"...
Who's "FLASHING through HER
    MENOPAUSE"???...

Helen weathered the blues and the blahs, and tried to put the happiest face on the long passage through a major life transition. On some days she felt chipper, on other ones she just needed to be alone. When she received an invitation from friends on one of her "down days," she answered with this starkly honest rhymed refusal:

SORRY... SORRY... I CAN'T ACCEPT...
But glad in a way I HAVE TO REJECT...
For I'm just as LOW as a CRAWLING SNAKE...
And just as TOUGH as an "OLD BULL STEAK"...
I'm just as FLAT as a WORN-DOWN HEEL...
And just as SOUR as an OLD LEMON PEEL...
I'd hate to INFLICT this "PUTRID STATE"
On such NICE FOLKS as YOU and YOUR MATE....

So far as Helen was concerned, it seemed that her body, which had served her so well for half a century, was suddenly failing on too many fronts at once. It was a sobering experience, and found expression in a note she sent to a sick friend.

It's sure upsetting what life can do
    and how it can mess up things for you...
We never know what's in store for us
    and it doesn't help to worry and fuss...
We just gotta take whatever life brings
    and as we grow older it brings "bad things"???

Helen
Steiner Rice
Ambassador
of Sunshine

I know from experience and it's no idle chatter
after "FORTY" there's always something the matter
Your BATTERY runs down and your MOTOR busts
Your CLUTCH starts to slip and your SPARK
    PLUGS rust...
Your CHASSIS cracks and you STRIP YOUR
    GEARS...
But we can't feel like TWENTY
When we've LIVED FIFTY YEARS???
...But we can't have the SUNSHINE without the
    RAIN
and we can't go through life without any pain...
We just gotta have both the BITTER and SWEET
for it takes them both to make life complete.

In spite of her own miseries, Helen was able to turn her misfortunes to good purpose in lifting the spirits of others. When J. R. Gibson was hospitalized for surgery during the summer of 1951, she wrote a poem wishing him a speedy recovery, and remarked in a post-script:

"Just had a double gum operation myself Monday, and my mouth feels like a 'dump truck' and all my teeth have 'little sweaters' on them . . .

> *So why should I sympathize with you???*
> *Gosh, you should feel 'superior'*
> *With not a single thing to do*
> *But rest on YOUR POSTERIOR????"*

Along with all of her other troubles, Helen, who had always been petite, for the first time in her life had to wrestle with her weight. "A Few Words from a Disillusioned Dieter" was a perfect example of Helen's ability to find humor in her own distress while comforting another woman caught up in the same struggle:

For breakfast it's EGGS
    and then STEAK at noon . . .
At night I "starve" on
    a "<u>WRINKLED PRUNE</u>" . . .
WHAT HAPPENS . . . ???
    Well, you'll never guess . . .
But when I stopped to
    buy a dress . . .
Instead of a <u>TEN</u>,
    did I get a <u>SURPRISE</u> . . .
I had <u>DIETED</u> into
    a <u>NUMBER 12 SIZE</u>???

As if weight-watching and menopause were not challenging enough, in early 1952, Helen began to suffer from a painful ailment ultimately diagnosed as a spastic colon. Confused and frustrated by new restrictions on her diet, she nonetheless remained feisty and lighthearted in explanations to her friends:

But these last months have sure been drastic . . .
    and now they say <u>MY COLON'S SPASTIC</u> . . .???
And at <u>MY AGE</u> ??? . . . with <u>HOT FLASHES</u>
    galore . . .
I'M back on "<u>BABY FOOD</u>" ONCE MORE . . .
Between us, it seems pretty "nutty"
    to fill my "tank" with "baby putty" . . .

When more health problems arose in November 1952, Helen wondered if God was testing her patience and resilience. She joked to her friend, Mary Dorman, that the jolt to her system may have come from Dwight Eisenhower's election as president.

> I guess the landslide victory was too much of a surprise shock to my nervous network, for I collapsed again??? and the Doctor ordered me to bed. Anyway I am glad the ELEPHANTS will be eating PEANUTS in the WHITE HOUSE again, for I was sick and tired of the JACK-ASSES BRAYING to the tune of the MISSOURI WALTZ.

In truth, Helen's physical illness and psychological disorientation were manifestations of a turning point in her life. Anyone suffering as Helen was might feel that God had deserted them. But Helen came to realize that the divine plan called for her to persevere, not give in to pain and self-pity. It was a choice that Helen's experiences had been leading her to since she was a little girl.

Reared in a home where prayer was as much a part of daily life as mealtime, Helen had, from youth, cultivated a highly personal relationship with God that continued into adulthood. It had seen her through the tragedy of Franklin's death and for years afterward eased the pain of many a solitary night in her room at the Gibson Hotel. The prayers and poems she wrote in the early 1950s, however, indicate that a powerful spiritual deepening was occurring in Helen. How to respond to incomprehensible forces—whether they came from a greed-driven postwar world, an unfeeling, mechanized society, the tragic fate of a friend, or the physical changes of midlife—was clearly at the core of Helen's questioning. In spite of her bewilderment, she seemed to understand that this time of disorientation was a stretching of the soul that came from God, and she expressed it poetically in December 1951:

> *It's hard for me to understand*
> *the bleakness of my spirit . . .*

I tell myself "THY WILL BE DONE" . . .
 And I know if I but bow my head
 and take what THOU HAST SENT . . .
 That I will walk again in the sun—
 But, filled with faith and unafraid,
 I still feel oddly strange . . .
 Why can I not be less aware
 Of the blight that has fallen
 and shrivelled my soul . . .
 When I know so well that YOU CARE?
 I am content . . . I do accept,
 and yet within me rises
 An aching hope that I may see
 Your face . . . not grave and saddened too . . .
 But "smiling" once again at me.

The same Helen who celebrated the Gibson centennial, crusaded to keep Carl Portune's job, cheered faceless thousands with her cards and dozens of friends with her letters, all the while joking openly about menopause and her diet, was privately trying to find her way out of the crucible of inner turmoil. Although she was unsophisticated in theology, her response to this spiritual desolation unconsciously repeated the solution adopted by Christian saints throughout the ages. She dedicated herself completely to an acceptance of a divine plan which Helen realized was far beyond her power of comprehension.

"God is at the beginning and the end of everything and there is nothing beyond HIM . . . so find comfort in that thought," she wrote, trying to console a grieving mother in September 1950. A year later, in July 1951, Helen sympathized with Dorothy Gradison on the death of her father, elaborating on the theme that the trials of life gave broader insights into its meaning:

I think of you so often, and always with sincere understanding of the difficult hours you have had to face during the last months. Having walked through so many "dark hours" myself, it makes me so keenly aware of the anxious uncertainty and emotional anguish you have been through and are experiencing. Somehow the little things that once seemed so important sink into insignificance as the deeper tragedies of life over-shadow them. Perhaps we establish our citizenship in Eternity, instead of in this restless world, and when we do that, we do all things so differently.

The practice Helen had cultivated for so long—cheering people through her letters and poems—was transformed in the 1950s into a personal ministry aimed at imparting spiritual counsel and compassion. Drawing on her personal experiences of pain, confusion, and depression, Helen conveyed to others a healing wisdom rooted in her own faith in God. She had many chances to share her newfound understanding of Christian truth. An especially poignant one occurred when Helen wrote to a woman confined in a tuberculosis sanitarium: "I have found that I am always comforted most in knowing that <u>OUR TOMORROWS</u> are in <u>ETERNAL HANDS</u> and they are <u>SAFE THERE</u>. . . ." In the context of Helen Steiner Rice's life, this sentiment stands as eloquent testimony both to the maturation of her character and the deepening of her personal spirituality.

Further evidence of the changes that redirected Helen's life in the postwar era is revealed by her verse diary. There, she compiled her daily prayers in poetic form, including the one that would later appear on the dedication page in her books. Everyone who appreciates Helen's work might think it was composed in the 1960s or 1970s, after Helen had achieved international fame, but in fact she wrote it on May 15, 1950.

> *Show me the way*
> *Not to Power or to Fame,*

Everything

Changes

Not to win laurels or praise for
My name . . .
But show me the way
To spread "The Great Story"
That Thine is the Kingdom,
The Power and Glory.

Her prayers indicate that Helen rededicated herself each day to being a means through which God could reach others, and her prayers were answered! Beginning in 1950, at the height of the Korean War, Helen's annual Christmas card showed the effects of her deeper experience of God. It conveyed her sincere affection for her friends, but at the same time the card was reflective:

. . . this year as we stand in the midst of war . . .
I asked, "Do we know what Christmas is for?" . . .
Christmas means PEACE, and the cards
*   we send . . .*
are filled with GOOD WISHES for family
*   and friend . . .*
and if we all practiced what Christmas cards say . . .
how could there be war and discord today . . .
why can't we LIVE CHRISTMAS,
*   EVERY DAY . . .*
why can't the SPIRIT OF CHRISTMAS stay . . .
why can't we be UNDERSTANDING
*   and KIND . . .*
why can't we see with OUR HEART,
*   not OUR MIND . . .*
the "VOICE OF CHRISTMAS" is pleading still . . .
for "PEACE ON EARTH—TO ALL MEN
*   OF GOOD WILL" . . .*

Nearly all the friends on her mailing list immediately recognized the wisdom of Helen's sentiments. Win Tice, a greeting card merchandiser, wrote to her from Chicago:

> I want to tell you how very much we all enjoyed your Christmas card. Your verse was one of the best I have ever read anywhere at anytime. I felt that it was so good that I read it aloud to an assembled group at Christmas time. It is sort of like reading Dickens at Christmas, you know. Some people say that long verses won't sell anymore, but I just have a sneaking notion that that would be a darn good seller if you cared to put your thoughts on the market. Maybe you don't want to commercialize your inner most thoughts, but should you, I think it would go very nicely.

With those few lines, Mr. Tice proved himself to be the first person to foresee that Helen's newfound power of spiritual self-expression could be a publishing bonanza. Others, however, were not far behind, for in a matter of months several friends and colleagues mentioned her talent for expressing profound religious truths in simple terms. Twice during 1951, prayer-poems composed by Helen were read on the television program, "Chapel of Dreams."

Inspiration comes from unknowable roots and is often expressed in unpredictable ways. What was to become one of Helen Steiner Rice's most famous poems about God is a perfect example. It was written during this period of self-discovery, but not as a greeting card verse. It first appeared in a letter to Della Seitz, a salesclerk at Mabley and Carew department store in Cincinnati. Later published in the Gibson newsletter in September 1951, it offers a remarkable window into the spiritual transformation which soon blossomed into a vocation of inspirational verse-writing for Helen.

> *I've never seen God,*
> *but I know how I feel . . .*

It's people like YOU
    who make HIM "SO REAL" . . .
My God is no stranger,
    HE'S friendly and gay . . .
And HE doesn't ask me
    to weep when I pray . . .
It seems that I pass HIM
    so often each day . . .
In the faces of people
    I meet on my way . . .
HE'S the stars in the heaven,
    a smile on some face . . .
A leaf on a tree
    or a rose in a vase . . .
HE'S winter and autumn
    and summer and spring . . .
In short, GOD IS EVERY
    REAL, WONDERFUL THING . . .
I wish I might meet HIM
    much more than I do . . .
I would if there were
    MORE PEOPLE LIKE YOU.

By December, the poem had circulated among Helen's friends at Gibson, and she received a growing number of requests for more copies. Fred Wagner, a young Gibson executive then working out of the Minneapolis office, received a copy from the company president. "I am looking forward to having it framed and put on the wall by my desk," Wagner wrote to Helen, continuing,

I would very much like to have another one for my home, and if it isn't asking too much, I wish you would send me another. It is so typical of you and everything you do and say. . . . We are anxiously awaiting your 1951 Christmas Card. I think it is the only one we ever save.

Other colleagues responded with equal enthusiasm, pressing for more copies of what coworker A. C. Stickney unabashedly described as "your masterpiece." "Certainly, Helen," his note concluded, "you possess a rare talent. . . ." Stickney compared Helen's verses to the poetry of Edgar Guest, for she had the "ability to put words together to express in a pleasing, yet clear, manner what we feel deep inside." He also pointed out that boxed assortment cards carrying Guest's verses were the top seller in West Coast retail stores.

Those who expected Helen's 1951 Christmas card to provide deep spiritual insight were not disappointed. That year's greeting card verse concentrated on the importance of friendship. In it, Helen explained that to understand the Christmas promise, it was necessary to relate to people, not just casually, but in a way that truly reflected the loving message of Christ:

Nothing I write the whole year through . . .
Means more to me than this card to YOU . . .
For you're more to me than a NAME and a FACE . . .
More than SOME ONE I met SOME PLACE . . .
You're one of Christ's messengers, sent to fulfill . . .
His Christmas promise of PEACE and GOOD WILL . . .
And He came at Christmas so we might find . . .
That it's not enough to be "casually kind" . . .
For life can only be PEACEFUL and GOOD . . .
When we are LOVED and UNDERSTOOD . . .
And there's only one way to understand . . .
And that's to follow Christ's "new command" . . .
"LOVE YE ONE ANOTHER AS I LOVED YOU" . . .
Not just as friends and acquaintances do . . .

For Christmas is more than a merry greeting . . .
Christ gave it to us as a "SPIRITUAL MEETING" . . .
So, blessed be the CHRISTMAS TIE that binds . . .
The love in our hearts to the thoughts in our minds . . .
And to those I've just met and to those I have known . . .
MERRY CHRISTMAS, GOD BLESS YOU and
  MAKE YOU HIS OWN.

One of the friends who received this card was a recovering alcoholic. The woman compared Helen's verse about the necessity of love and understanding to the spiritual message of Alcoholics Anonymous' Twelve Step program, and told Helen that she had used the card's sentiments in two recent talks:

> I don't suppose when you wrote this card that you ever dreamed that it would be used to encourage, inspire and help a bunch of ex-drunks who represent a cross-section of life—from top drawer to skid row. And I thought you might like to know that you have not only my sincere thanks but the thanks of many other AAs. . . .
>
>   We always ask for comments after the meeting and one man said, "I don't believe I can say anything right now. I'm still thinking about that Christmas card." This particular man happens to be a top architect in the city.

On February 8, 1952, Mildred Miller, a columnist for the *Cincinnati Enquirer*, printed the poem, "God and You," which had so excited Helen's fellow employees at Gibson. Response to the article was overwhelming. "Brooding about the treachery and villainy of our time has almost killed hope within me," wrote one reader, who complimented Helen for writing "far enough above the rivalries and vicious jealousies of commercialized religion to speak in terms of universal truth." Others wrote either to Gibson executives or Helen herself expressing similar feelings. Most of

Helen
Steiner Rice
Ambassador
of Sunshine

them asked where Gibson cards carrying the verse might be purchased, but no such greeting cards existed.

Helen pursued her ever-expanding spiritual ministry in more private ways, continuing to write letters of comfort, encouragement, and condolence that made a real difference in the lives of their recipients. Those letters were often passed along to others who benefited from Helen's insights. What she communicated was an eternal truth—the all-embracing nature of God's love, which linked people everywhere to one another. It struck a sympathetic chord in everyone, for the sentiment conveyed a message people wanted to hear, one that was clearer because Helen transmitted it with great conviction. "The name Helen Steiner Rice goes down in my memory book," Dorothy Meyer, a recently widowed friend, wrote in July 1953. "I shall always remember people like you who gave so much of themselves to Bob. . . . Your wonderful encouraging letters he treasured always and they are still in there in his drawer. . . . You and I loved Bob. You as a <u>dear,</u> <u>dear friend</u> and I as his wife. You shall always be near to me in my thoughts and memories."

As time passed, the accolades grew in number. Even though she was pleased by these compliments, Helen seemed to feel that she was not doing enough to recognize God's blessings. Struggling with an awareness of her own inadequacy, Helen bared her soul in a letter-poem she wrote in February 1953:

> *. . . I've been so discouraged with my "faltering ways"*
> *and disheartened over my "wasted days" . . .*
> *I've prayed that "my heart might sing" once more,*
> *and allow me to do things I've done before . . .*
> *Without a HELPLESS, INADEQUATE FEELING*
> *that makes me fall to my knees appealing . . .*

That I may "BETTER PAY MY WAY"
Instead of feeling at the end of the day
That I have failed in more ways than one
To get the deeds of service done
That I had wanted so much to do
and hoped that God would see me through....

In the midst of her spiritual turmoil, Helen decided to follow the message of her heart, which told her to make a visit back home to Lorain in the autumn of 1953. It was a wise choice, for it gave her an opportunity to look through the memorabilia she had saved during her early days in business. Reminiscing over her souvenirs, Helen was profoundly moved by how clearly they pointed toward the transformation then occurring within her. She expressed her feelings to a friend in a verse about self-discovery:

And I never come "home" and search through the attic—
but what I am "lifted to regions ecstatic"—
For with mirth that is quietly chuckling inside
I realize that way back then on "The Crest of the Tide"
I knew not a "smidgeon" of "real values" because—
I was far too enthralled by the "phony applause" ...
Of course, way back then I was sure that I knew—
Just what to say and
Just what to do—

If knowing what to say was ever a problem for Helen Steiner Rice, it was a well-kept secret. When, for example, Gertrude Steiner alerted her sister to the illness of a member of the Twentieth Street Methodist Church in Lorain, Helen was quick to respond with alliterative observations:

> I think this pressure and push and tension and turmoil and terrific tempo that we are traveling today is disturbing our emotions. And no matter how we try to escape the increasing "clouds of chaos and confusion and conflict" that gather on all sides, we are caught in the "web." But when the going gets too tough and I recognize MY HELPLESSNESS, then I just turn it all over to God. . . .

Somehow, the right words seemed to come to Helen even in situations where spiritual matters were not foremost. On New Year's Day, 1954, she tried to phone Gertrude to let her know that she would be out that evening. Helen was unsuccessful, partly as a result of operator error but also because of the rudeness of someone who stayed on the Lorain party line too long. When Gertrude was unable to reach Helen at the scheduled time, she had the hotel initiate a search for her sister. Furious at the "commotion, anxiety and hullabaloo" that had been caused by "the sheer stupidity and casual carelessness" of the telephone operators, Helen wrote imperiously to the president of the Lorain Telephone Company:

> FIRST OFF . . . AS OF NOW . . . AND NOT TOMORROW OR THE NEXT DAY, BUT THIS VERY INSTANT . . . I wish to have the telephone at 2714 Reid Avenue . . . put on a MAIN LINE, for I never again intend to subject myself to such an ORDEAL as I went through on January the first.

No doubt Helen's loneliness—the feeling of desolation that arose from sitting in a hotel room on New Year's Day unable to contact her only close relative—contributed to her uncharacteristically angry reaction.

On another occasion, Helen was having difficulty getting shoes to match her custom-made hats and costumes. The St. Louis company from which she had previously ordered up to five pairs of

shoes at a time—"purples, kelly greens, chartreuses and grays"—
failed to fill an order placed in February 1954. By the end of April,
Helen's fury at the delay matched her anger about the Lorain
party line, and she had no qualms about letting the company's
president know how she felt:

PLEASE TELL ME, WILL YOU PEOPLE CONTINUE TO
MAKE SHOES FOR ME? I would like to have my shoes as well
recognized and publicized as my hats, and I maintain that a woman
is always well dressed if her two extremities are "eye-catchers!" . . .
. . . I think your shoes are just superb, and you must be the
POWER behind the HIGH-POWERED SHOES that all pulchri-
tudinous women love . . . and, with your artistic sensitivity and your
creative ability, you just cannot turn a deaf ear to my letter.

Helen Steiner Rice instinctively knew when to fight for herself,
but she seemed to relish the prospect of fighting for others. On
one occasion, a favorite clergyman was suddenly relieved of his
duties as pastor of her church in Cincinnati. Helen soon learned
that when he departed, a tape recorder she had contributed for his
personal use was left behind. She immediately took the matter up
with the board of trustees, and the tape recorder was soon delivered to the minister at his new parish house.

Whatever pleasure she derived from her spiritual growth and
service to her friends was, however, mitigated by work at Gibson,
which seemed to be progressively more demanding. In November
1954, Helen confided to a friend: "I have been pushing so much
work into TOMORROW, that when TOMORROW comes, it is
so filled up with YESTERDAYS, that I have no TODAY to work
in. It seems to be a universal disease that is destroying mankind."
Helen understandably felt a great deal of strain, for while her work
as editor at Gibson Art claimed most of her time, her fame was
rapidly spreading because of the inspirational verses and personal
Christmas cards she sent to friends. Radio personalities read them

over the air to enhance broadcasts, and as time passed, Helen found herself constantly granting requests to use her poems for devotional programs.

By May 1955, Helen had grown philosophical enough about this turn of events to be able to write to Vera Schmalstig, a friend in Dayton, with a sense of relief:

"I am ANOTHER YEAR OLDER . . . ANOTHER HAIR GRAYER . . . AND ANOTHER TOOTH LOOSER, but, Darlin', being 55 was much easier than being 45 . . . maybe I have stopped resisting the inevitable . . . for

> *. . . TIME CANNOT BE HALTED*
> *In its SWIFT and ENDLESS FLIGHT . . .*
> *For AGE is sure to follow YOUTH*
> *As DAY comes after NIGHT . . .*
> *And while being young and frivolous*
> *Was very stimulating . . .*
> *I find that being OLD and WISE???*
> *Is very COMPENSATING!"*

A few months later, in September 1955, Helen's wisdom made its way into a Miami Beach newspaper when she predicted that the country would someday see a woman president. She had gone to Florida with Gertrude and a friend, partly to visit a cousin and also to relax. Helen admitted, however, to a newspaper reporter that "relaxing is difficult for one with my energy." She eventually sent a copy of the article to Edith Wilker, her former teacher and mentor, whom she credited with inspiring all of her students to pursue lofty goals and set high standards. Mrs. Wilker responded enthusiastically:

The clipping you enclose indicates that you are still the same Helen in spite of the intervening years—full of vim and vigor. Best of all,

Helen (in white hat) gave the opening remarks at a fashion show in 1956 at the invitation of Gibson vice president Fred Wagner (seated at Helen's left).

life has apparently not robbed you of ambition and idealism, usually the first virtues to succumb to time and tide. . . . You may even land in the President's chair yourself. You would, I'm sure, steer clear of many of the mistakes of recent years which are responsible for our present anxieties.

While Helen never seriously considered a political career, flattered though she may have been by Wilker's suggestion, a return to public speaking held a certain appeal. She was committed to the idea that the world's only hope rested with individual acts of kindness, and the public forum offered a chance to convey that message with maximum effect.

As fate would have it, the opportunity to communicate Helen's inspirational message presented itself just a few months later, in the autumn of 1956. Fred Wagner, the Gibson executive from Minneapolis who had admired Helen's poem, "God and You," had been recently transferred to Cincinnati. He was placed in charge of finding a speaker to address a luncheon for the wives of members of

Helen
Steiner Rice
*Ambassador
of Sunshine*

the National Association of Retail Druggists, who were meeting in Cincinnati for a convention. Wagner's coworkers suggested that he ask Helen Steiner Rice.

Helen eagerly accepted Wagner's invitation to address the "style show luncheon" for eight hundred women in the Netherland Hotel's glamorous "Hall of Mirrors." After Wagner's flattering introductory remarks, Helen modestly and charmingly greeted everyone:

> *I'd like to chat for an hour or two*
> *And personally welcome each one of you,*
> *But time goes by on jet-propelled wings*
> *And I'm just an* <u>OPENER</u> *for MUCH NICER*
> *THINGS . . .*

Although Helen knew she was only the "opening act" for the fashion show, she apparently lost track of time once she stepped in front of the microphone. Fred Wagner recalled that after half an hour, "she was just getting warmed up." Even though the audience was "enthralled with her," another Gibson executive whispered to Fred that someone had to stop Helen. Ever the diplomat, Wagner devised a gentle way to end her enthusiastic speech. This encounter marked the beginning of a working relationship that often placed Fred Wagner in the position of Helen's adversary. He summarized the connection, which spanned a quarter of a century, with admiration: "You can't say anything derogatory about Helen Steiner Rice—although Helen and I fought like cats and dogs for many years, we turned out to be the very best of friends."

Through all the years she worked at Gibson, Helen had lived in downtown Cincinnati, just a few blocks from her place of employment. A small hotel room overlooking the city's cement and black-top heart was hardly the life Helen Steiner Rice envisioned for herself when she married Franklin in 1929, but she had come to accept it. Despite its disadvantages, her home was, after all, close to every necessary convenience and within easy walking distance to work. Helen thought that the little security she derived from her restricted urban world would continue forever. She was mistaken. In 1956, when Gibson moved to a new plant in suburban Amberley Village, a new era dawned. The loss of proximity between home and work required Helen to make one more change in a decade of adjustments. After the move, she had to rely on a special company bus to transport her, along with dozens of other Gibson Art employees, to the new facility. She boarded the bus each morning, put a little white towel over the seat behind the driver, and took her place among her fellow commuters..

She lamented the inconvenience of the new arrangement to Edith Wilker, who assured her that commuting at an early hour was "one of those experiences which cure, if they do not kill." Mrs. Wilker also addressed a matter of greater importance—Helen's writing—for she had read recent verses Helen sent and liked what she saw. "Apparently the move has interfered in no way with your creative power," she commented after reading a "beautiful poem" she had just received from Helen. "Who knows?" she quipped, "that early-morning inspiration may give rise to others just as fine."

As ever, Edith Wilker's words influenced Helen. After mulling over Edith's remarks, Helen reconsidered her daily routine, and soon began the practice of pausing each morning before she entered the Gibson offices to make her personal meditations for the day. Her creative writing flourished. "Have you ever published your poems in book form?" a friend wrote early in 1957. "If not as yet, surely you will some-time; these beautiful thoughts and words are much too lovely not to be enjoyed by every-one. If you have; please let me know what you call the book, and where I can buy a copy."

Despite her growing fame, Helen's inspirational poems remained limited in circulation. Still, by 1957, such poems as "Let Us Keep

Christ in Christmas" had appeared in many church bulletins and newspapers. At the same time, individuals such as Harry Bailey, from faraway Lowestoft, England, created their own Christmas cards based on Helen's verses and offered payment in return for the opportunity to reprint her poems. It began to seem obvious that Helen's talent for writing upbeat spiritual messages deserved more attention. As she grew more frustrated by demonstrations of cruelty and stupidity in the world around her, Helen continued to nurse the opinion that the solution to the world's problems lay not in technology or institutional religion, but in spreading the eternal message of love. In time, Helen came to believe that God had cast her in the role of showing how loving behavior could be part of everyday life, but she did not yet know how to play the part.

Everything
Changes

7

To
Spread
"The
Great
Story"

$\mathcal{Y}$ou really have more verbal bounce to the ounce than anyone we have ever known," Elwood's son, Ernest Rice, wrote to Helen in 1958, "but we also realize that it stems from an enlarged heart. I guess, that like all other muscles, the heart grows with use, and that certainly applies to you." Ernest, then president of the Burdell Oil Company, was only a few years younger than Helen. He had been present at her marriage to Franklin nearly thirty years earlier, and, over the years, had paid close attention to the many accomplishments of his "favorite aunt."

Ernest's appreciation of Helen's talent for buoying up the spirits of others was not unique. While visiting Helen's cousin, Hulda Cron, in an Indiana nursing home, Dorothy Miller had read Helen's cards and notes to the elderly lady. Afterward, Dorothy reported Hulda's stirring response to Helen:

> She glowed and she wept. She wanted me to tell you that a tear in the eye could be a blessing. She spoke of you with deep affection. She feels security in your concern for her . . . she remembers and cherishes the thought that you are keeping in touch with her.

Cincinnati Enquirer reporter Mildred Miller described Helen in the newspaper as "one of my favorite people," noting that "Her face is radiant, her voice effervescent, her eyes sparkling, her manner charming." Subsequently, Mrs. Miller featured vignettes about Helen in many of her articles. In September 1958, for example, Helen wrote a poetic thank-you note to a salesclerk at a millinery shop after the woman cheerfully exchanged a hat for her. Unknown to Helen, the shop's owner sent the verse to Mildred Miller, who based a column on the rhymed acknowledgment. No one knew it at the time, but that note would ultimately become the basis for Helen Steiner Rice's famous poem, "Heart Gifts":

> *It's not the things that can be bought . . .*
> *That are life's richest treasure . . .*
> *It's priceless little courtesies . . .*
> *That money cannot measure . . .*
> *It's some little act of graciousness . . .*
> *Or some kindly little favor . . .*
> *That fills the heart with gratitude . . .*
> *And leaves memories to savor . . .*
> *And a very good example . . .*
> *Was a recent hat transaction . . .*
> *That warmed my heart sincerely . . .*
> *And left a nice reaction!*

After that, Helen and Mrs. Miller began to exchange ideas. On one occasion, Helen told Mrs. Miller that she thought all children should hear the German legend of "The Christmas Guest," which Helen remembered Grandma Bieri telling her when she was a child. Inspired by the simple honesty of the tale and convinced that this story of ministering to Christ through others would be a "best-seller," Mrs. Miller printed Helen's rhymed summary of it in December 1958. She later noted that greeting card dealers had underestimated the item's potential popularity. Response from

Mrs. Miller's readers was so great that two weeks later it prompted a follow-up column:

> Many women wrote or telephoned, begging for information where they could purchase the card, saying they had gone to one store after another in search of it—but to no avail. Several revealed that in desperation they had clipped out the column and were mailing it in lieu of a Christmas card.

As Helen's inspirational verses grew in popularity, their commercial possibilities rose in the estimation of the executives at Gibson. Her friend Bill Dresmann, in charge of product creation, approached Helen about signing some of her more successful cards, and soon her name appeared on numerous Gibson offerings. Her personal Christmas cards, however, continued to draw the warmest reaction—a "grass roots" response that had nothing to do with corporate marketing—and they contributed immeasurably to the public's appreciation of Helen Steiner Rice as an inspirational poet.

"What a wonderful paradise this world would be if every one would let themselves be a radiating center for God's Love," wrote one woman after receiving Helen's personal card. "If I were to imitate anyone I know it would be you. Not for the clothes, but that warm, kindly smile and sunshine that just peps and invigorates those you meet." Mildred Miller echoed that lady's private sentiment in her column when she printed another one of Helen's cards in its entirety. She described Helen as "a veritable year-'round 'Mary Christmas,'" adding that "Her adherence to the highest ideals, ever readiness to soothe troubled hearts and her rare capacity to radiate sunshine wherever she goes, have won her the title of 'Angel' from those touched by her 'magic wand.'"

Mildred Miller's admiration of Helen's work was not simply that of a local columnist praising a hometown artist; the evidence makes it clear that Helen was widely appreciated as a new voice. One of Gibson's executives in Minneapolis, for instance, wrote to Helen that her card had been read on television there as the Christmas message from the Gibson dealers who sponsored the program. Clearly, the inspirational card itself was becoming more popular, but greeting card manufacturers could not yet see Helen Steiner Rice's simple, poignant message as the wave of the future.

Always a curious blend of creative artist and businesswoman, Helen proved to be ahead of her employers; she had already been surveying the marketability of inspirational messages. Using the occasion of a trip home to Lorain in the autumn of 1959, Helen undertook "a little private-eye work" at local greeting card establishments. She visited seven retail shops, checked over their displays, and talked business with the owners. The project recalled her earliest assignments at Gibson Art, for upon her return to Cincinnati, Helen submitted a report to three Gibson executives, commenting that "whenever I see a greeting card installation I am like an old circus horse smelling the sawdust."

Helen felt enlightened and invigorated by her study, for it convinced her that "Even in creative work you can't afford to be an 'ISOLATIONIST' and stay chained to your desk . . . you have to circulate to keep the blood of genius and imagination flowing through the artery of productivity." Worried by what she observed, Helen recommended "more contacts with the outside for key creative people," noting that "the best results are always obtained when the sales and the creative meet each other on the common ground of understanding." In a letter to Fred Wagner, Helen reflected, "I used to think, with my own little pen, pencil and typewriter, that I could win the American heart, but I realize now that so much enters into this highly competitive game before the customer even sees the card and . . . my question is not WHY DON'T WE SELL MORE but HOW DO WE SELL AS MUCH AS WE DO, with competition as keen and wily and impenetrable as NIKITA [Khrushchev] himself." Only one of the stores Helen visited in Lorain had a special display of inspirational cards, and it was put up by a Gibson competitor.

One of the Gibson inspirational cards that carried Helen's byline was a Christmas greeting that included a verse entitled "The Priceless Christmas Gift." Written in July 1957, it first appeared in the Gibson Christmas line of 1958, selling for thirty-five cents. So successful that it was reissued for the next two years, the verse eventually made its way into the hands of a television personality in December 1960, and changed Helen Steiner Rice's life forever.

Lawrence Welk's connection with Helen may well have given rise to the most important advance in her career. It originated with Aladdin Pallante, a performer on Welk's nationally televised program. Aladdin, as he was known, was an accomplished violinist, singer, and comedian who also did interpretive recitations. Aladdin's sister sent him a Christmas card bearing the verse, "The Priceless Gift of Christmas." When he read it, Aladdin instantly recognized the power of the message:

Christmas is a heavenly gift
that only God can give,
It's ours just for the asking
for as long as we shall live.
This priceless gift of Christmas
is meant just for the heart,
And we receive it only
when we become a part
Of the kingdom and the glory
which is ours to freely take,
For God sent the Holy Christ Child
at Christmas for our sake . . .
This priceless gift of Christmas

Helen
Steiner Rice
Ambassador
of Sunshine

is within the reach of all—
The rich, the poor, the young and old,
the greatest and the small.
So take His priceless gift of love,
reach out and you receive,
And the only payment that God asks
is just that you believe.

Aladdin approached Lawrence Welk about using it on the air during the holiday season, and Welk approved. On December 17, 1960, Aladdin gave a dramatic rendering of the poem before a nationwide audience; the effect was astonishing.

Positive reaction to Aladdin's reading overwhelmed the staff in Lawrence Welk's office. It was the kind of "hit" that turns competent television performers into "stars," and demand proved so great that before year's end the poem was repeated on the show. Sensing a bonanza, Welk's associates first sought Helen's permission to turn the poem into a song. Helen innocently responded on January 4, 1961, "If you feel there is a possibility for reaching more people through the medium of song, who am I to restrain you? God gave the verses to me, and I want to give them to the world."

Lawrence Welk was thunderstruck. A savvy businessman and television veteran, he wrote to Helen on January 11: "What a marvelous world this would be, if more people shared your views. It was a genuine pleasure to find a letter like yours among the many thousand we receive each week." Welk urged George Cates, his musical director, to set her poem to music. He also instructed his music publisher to send Helen a contract that would secure rights to use "The Priceless Gift of Christmas." Afterwards, he asked to review other verses Helen had written that might be considered for a proposed album of recitations Aladdin had done on the show.

Helen was flattered by Welk's idea, telling him that his suggestion left her "deeply touched, a little awed, and very humble." Still, it was not the temptation of personal recognition that moved her, but rather some instinct she needed to follow. As Helen put it, partly in rhyme:

> . . . I feel so "certain-sure" (just as I have these long, hard years that I have fought for the survival of this type of sentiment against what I term sophisticated vulgarity) that if you decide to make an album of Aladdin's readings that together we will be putting into the reach of searching souls and groping hands "hyacinths for the soul." For all of us are PILGRIMS here . . . searching for a word of cheer, groping for a ray of light . . . to make our "pilgrimage" more bright . . . yearning to be understood . . . so we may find that life is good!

Helen agreed to give Welk a number of verses that were "suitable for the seasons that are immediately approaching,"—Valentine's Day, Easter, and Mother's Day. She also told him that she had received his contract from the Harry Von Tilzer Music Publishing Company granting permission to put "The Priceless Gift" to music. "I have only a very limited knowledge of contracts," Helen wrote to Welk, "but a very large admiration for you, so I sign without studying it."

Both Lawrence Welk and Aladdin were extremely curious about the talented woman with whom they were dealing; so much so that Welk arranged to meet Helen during a promotional tour that included a stop in Cincinnati. Fate brought them together in June 1961, when Lawrence Welk performed at Cincinnati Gardens. Welk and Aladdin invited Helen to dinner, and they were overjoyed when she accepted. During the meal, Helen mentioned to Aladdin that she was working on a new poem for a friend, Dora Fischer, who needed a verse for her church's convention. Dora had asked Helen if she knew the story of Albrecht Dürer's life and the sacrifices made by a friend to ensure his success. Dora had suggested this as the theme for the poem. Aladdin immediately expressed an interest in the project, and requested a copy of the poem when Helen finished it.

Helen completed the poem and, in August 1961, Dora presented it to a Bible conference in Holland, Michigan. It was called "The Praying Hands." The poem was so powerful that convention-goers eagerly snatched up the two thousand available copies. Happy to have pleased her friend, Helen failed to grasp the importance of her achievement. She also forgot about Aladdin's request to read the verse when it was finished.

Involved with her work and absorbed in the lives of her friends, Helen was surprised when the phone rang on November 15, 1961, and she heard Aladdin's voice. He was calling long distance; he wanted to know if he could read the poem she had described the night they had dinner in Cincinnati on Lawrence Welk's Thanksgiving show. Amazed that he remembered and flattered by the suggestion, Helen agreed without hesitation. The next day she sent Aladdin a telegram verifying her commitment, and then followed up with a letter that included a copy of "The Praying Hands." The letter included a personal poem for Aladdin:

> *Aladdin, it is folks like YOU*
> *Who take the "little things I do"*
> *And by some magic trick of fate*
> *MY LITTLE THINGS seem almost*
> *   "GREAT" . . .*
> *And in my heart I realize*
> *It's not that I am "smart" or "wise" . . .*
> *It's just that God through folks like you*
> *BREATHES LIFE into the things I do,*
> *And far beyond my power of seeing*
> *In "HIM I MOVE and HAVE MY BEING!"*

After her poem, "The Praying Hands," was read by Aladdin on "The Lawrence Welk Show" in 1961, the popularity of Helen's work soared.

In her wildest dreams, Helen Steiner Rice could never have gauged the impact of her casual agreement to let Aladdin read "The Praying Hands."

On November 18, 1961, Helen flew home to Lorain to spend the Thanksgiving holidays with Gertrude. That night Helen and her sister saw Aladdin read the poem on Lawrence Welk's show. They were pleased with the performance, but never suspected it would provoke such an enthusiastic response. Within hours, the Welk and Gibson offices were deluged with requests for copies of what viewers thought was a Gibson greeting card. Unfortunately for Gibson, already well into the competitive Christmas season, no such card existed. Taken completely off guard, Gibson worked frantically to meet demands for the verse. The company had special copies printed and included with them a note that "The Praying Hands" card would be introduced into Gibson's inspirational Christmas line in 1962. Helen Steiner Rice had evidently tapped a deeply felt spiritual vein among people who needed to find meaning in the sacrifices of their everyday lives.

In the days after Aladdin's reading, thousands of requests poured in from churches, social agencies, schools, and other organizations, all asking to reprint the poem, buy it, or use it in one way or another. A school principal in Farley, Iowa, wanted to make "The Praying Hands" a part of his speech course; a Canadian com-

"The Praying Hands" became one of the most popular greeting cards ever issued.

pany in the province of Quebec appealed for permission to have it translated into French. Helen's friend, Mildred Miller, sagely anticipated the public demand and printed "The Praying Hands" in her *Cincinnati Enquirer* column.

While Helen was understandably excited about all the recognition, she claimed no personal credit for her amazing success. "DO NOT ASK ME TO EXPLAIN IT," she later wrote to a friend who also aspired to be a writer:

> . . . most everything I ever wrote silently slipped into oblivion. . . but then one day God, who had been arranging the SCENERY ALL MY LIFE . . . just dropped one little unknown verse in the pathway of Aladdin . . . I had nothing to do with it. . . . YOU CAN'T EXPLAIN GOD . . . YOU JUST HAVE TO FOLLOW HIM and know that HE NEVER MAKES ANY MISTAKES.

Those professionally associated with Helen did not want to make any mistakes either. Eager to benefit from such conspicuous success, Aladdin sought and received permission from Helen to read another one of her poems, "Prayer for Peace," on Mr. Welk's Christmas show. Equally anxious not to miss out on a potential merchandising coup, Gibson formulated plans to bring out "The Praying Hands" card not only in its Christmas and Easter lines, but in other offerings as well. One Gibson memo urged the sales force:

> The "Praying Hands" design may well prove to be the "hottest thing in the line" that we've had for years. Every indication so far points to that kind of a success. DON'T MISS PUSHING THIS "HOT NUMBER" STRONGLY . . . IT'S A MONEY MAKER!

Thanks largely to the success of "The Praying Hands," a January 1962 *Cincinnati Enquirer* article profiled Helen Steiner Rice, proclaiming, "Woman Greeting Card Editor Considers God Her

'First Boss.'" In just a few words, it captured the firmly God-centered viewpoint that directed Helen's life. For years, she had begun each day with prayer, surrendering herself and her talents to whatever plan the Lord had laid out for her, and repeating the words of personal devotions she had written. She asked God for the courage to recognize her own failings and forgive the short-comings of others. "I'm not ashamed to witness for Him. And I don't care who knows it, in the business world or in the social world," Helen told reporter Libby Lackman. Judging from the phenomenal sales of her writings, her message was one that people were eager to hear.

Encouraged by the public reception of Helen's verses, a Gibson card retailer in Canton, Ohio, arranged to have her appear on a radio talk show called "Bill Karenbar's Bee-Line." The hour-long appearance was originally proposed as a question and answer show, with Helen responding to inquiries about the greeting card indus-try. In an insightful assessment of Helen's strengths and weak-nesses, Gibson's director of public relations, Lee Greenwell, won-dered whether Helen, whose genius he never questioned, might strain the limits of that format with her unbridled enthusiasm. He wrote in a memo of March 9, 1962:

> As you know, Helen is quite a talker and once she gets started on the subject of greeting cards and how important they are in our lives to build friendship, bring happiness and make this world a bet-ter place because of thoughtfulness, you sit spellbound at her sin-cerity . . . she always has a message really worth listening to.

Greenwell's instincts were correct. By the time the arrange-ments were finalized, Helen was preparing "to give an informal lit-tle talk about GOD . . . GREETING CARDS . . . and GUIDED MISSILES," and to read some of her verses that had been featured on the Welk Show.

Seventeen northern Ohio newspapers were notified of Helen's scheduled appearance, and her friends in Lorain made sure that they could pick up the Canton radio station. The minister of the Methodist church Helen attended when she was in Lorain even helped spread the word by announcing her radio appearance from the pulpit. Gertrude Steiner later told her sister that the minister said "people would like to know about it 'cause they were proud to have you as a member of their church." Ever astute, Gertrude suggested that Helen's recent two-thousand-dollar contribution to the church might have influenced the pastor's support. She dryly noted: "I think you pleased him so much with your contribution he is trying to plug your work for you. . . ."

Helen had no more ardent fan than her lifelong friend, Isabel Bloedorn, who fiddled constantly with two radios before she found the "Bee-Line" program. Helen was scheduled for the two to three p.m. slot, and "Issy" left herself a mere six minutes to get to a three o'clock funeral, just so she could hear as much of Helen's talk as possible. "I heard every bit of the description of your attire," she wrote Helen afterwards; ". . . your answers to the questions relative to your years with the Gibson Art Company—your reading of the Praying Hands . . . you did wonderful, and I was so glad I was able to get to hear you." Gertrude Steiner, Isabel's neighbor, found "Issy's" delight amusing. She later told Helen, "I never saw her so pleased about anything, she was waiting for me at the side door, and she said, 'Guess what! I got Helen's program and heard it all.'"

Her generous spirit seemed to invite requests from others, and Helen always found it hard to say no. Following John Glenn's historic space flight in February 1962, for example, his mother, Clara, was named "World Mother" of 1962. Mrs. Glenn's close friend, Inez Lashley, asked Helen to write a poem honoring Clara that could be presented to her by admirers in New Concord, Ohio. Happy to oblige, Helen penned "A Mother's Day Tribute to John

Glenn's Mother," which was presented to Clara Glenn in a touching ceremony. It was widely reprinted in newspapers, and without Helen's knowledge was sent to Aladdin, who read it with astounding effect on Lawrence Welk's Mother's Day show.

Just as Helen was generous with her talents and time, she was equally bighearted with her financial resources. She was a liberal contributor to Christ Methodist Church in Lorain, where she retained membership despite her residence in Cincinnati. She also participated in activities like the fund drive to build a new church, and helped provide furnishings for it. Her generosity inspired George Bender, then pastor at Christ Methodist, to remark that he was as grateful to encounter "a soul which delights in its duty to the First Boss" as he was to receive her offering.

Closer to home, Helen learned that no major benefactors had come forward from the congregation of Wesley Chapel—her place of worship in downtown Cincinnati—to underwrite the renovation and restoration of that historic Methodist church. Consequently, she decided to do something about it. Sending a sizeable contribution to Herbert Frazer, who was Wesley Chapel's minister in August 1962, she made a greater impact on him than she had on Reverend Bender. Expressing appreciation for Helen's financial contribution, Frazer praised Helen's unexpected support of his ministry:

> Your presence in the congregation, your faithfulness in your attendance, your smile, your evidence of attention to my poor sermons, and the greeting at the conclusion of the services are all so meaningful to me.

That inner radiance, which George Bender and Herbert Frazer easily recognized, also fascinated many others; it was part of Helen's compelling personality. After Helen appeared before the National Secretaries Association, one woman wrote that she was nearly moved to tears just watching Helen read verses: "I don't know how to say how I appreciated the beauty of soul we were permitted to see last evening." Similar letters came in from people who never met Helen, but still were deeply moved by her poetry. One was sent by a teenager in New Jersey who was recovering from surgery for a brain tumor. The operation had left her physically handicapped and terribly discouraged, but the strength she drew from Helen's poems made all the difference in the world. She wrote: "I believe that when a person is so depressed and doesn't know where to turn, a spiritual poem, like yours, can sometimes show them the way, far better than a preacher could ever explain." One of Helen's old friends put it best when she commented: "When I read the things you have written, I always think—'Helen is indeed in touch with the Infinite.'"

The popularity of Helen's inspirational cards spiraled ever upward during 1962. As might be expected, Gibson's executives welcomed predictions that a Christmas set of Helen's verses might sell a million copies, so they began planning for such an eventuality early in the year. Since booklets, stationery, plaques, and wall-hangings based on Helen's verses were, like her greeting cards, selling throughout the year, Gibson's West Coast subsidiary, Buzza, began to offer an eight-foot-long "Helen Steiner Rice Boutique" of inspirational merchandise to retailers. Buzza's promotional literature, describing Helen as "America's beloved verse writer," pinpointed in a few words why she was so popular:

> She writes from the heart and for people in all walks of life. A keen student of human nature, she writes simply, expressing thoughts and ideas that many have felt but cannot always put into words. While few people know what today's sophisticated poets are trying to say, everyone understands and loves the work of Mrs. Rice. More than anything else, the underlying message of her verses is that the only really important values are the basic virtues of trust, honor and love.

By 1962, it was apparent that Helen Steiner Rice's inspirational verses had become "big business" for the company now known as Gibson Greetings. Helen often advanced the opinion that Gibson Greetings, "through no conscious effort on their part have become the 'PERFECT CHANNEL' for distribution" of the work that belonged to her and to God. Helen believed and steadfastly claimed that she retained sole ownership of her poems. Gibson executives predictably felt a sense of co-ownership by virtue of Helen's employment with them as an editor who also authored greeting card messages. What might have become a messy dispute was resolved because both Helen and Gibson Greetings acknowledged that each had more to gain through cooperation than conflict.

While Helen often expressed embarrassment at what she called the "crudely commercial" advertising and merchandising policies pursued by Gibson, those very efforts helped boost sales in a way she could never have imagined. For example, in 1963 Gibson capitalized on Helen's relationship with Lawrence Welk, obtaining permission to use Welk's photograph in advertising inspirational cards and softbound collections of Helen's verses. Three of the four pages in the Gibson Retailing Digest distributed at the 1963 New York Stationery Show featured the inspirational line that was "seen and heard coast to coast" on the Lawrence Welk Show.

Gibson's card sales undoubtedly benefited from the Welk connection, but there were friends and admirers of Helen Steiner Rice who maintained that Welk also gained a greater audience share because people wanted to hear Helen's verses read on the air. One was Goebel Thompson, a former bellman at the Gibson Hotel. A humble man, he was awed by Helen's friendliness to him and followed her career with devotion. When his health failed, and he was hospitalized, Helen wrote to him regularly. In July 1963, he assured Helen that, as a result of her poems, "the Lawrence Welk Show has picked up more viewers in its vast audience than they will ever realize." In another touching letter, Mr. Thompson described the scene at the sanitarium when the patients were permitted to watch the Welk show and Helen's name was mentioned:

> . . . to think an old bellman in a T. B. hospital can get up and shout—That lady who you speak of is my Friend, and Friend to so many bellmen and people it would take the hour show for a fellow like me to tell the world just what a person Mrs. Rice really is, I mean a lady who commands respect, is respected, and respects each person regardless of race, color, religion or anything one can think of. . . .

Thompson prayed that God would bless Helen so she could continue to "put words together for folks like us to understand."

His sentiments were closely aligned with Helen's, for she truly believed that her amazing success was because God was directing all her efforts. If any proof of God's approval of her mission was needed, it came in July 1963. A booklet of her verses, entitled "Just for You," was published and devoured by the public. By October, it had sold nearly 500,000 copies. Now keenly sensitive to the power of Helen Steiner Rice's message, Gibson began advertising in church papers and reaped immediate rewards.

By November 1963, Helen's confidence in her relationship with Lawrence Welk had reached such a point that she could request that Aladdin read her poem, "One Nation Under God," on the Thanksgiving show. "Personally, I have felt very deeply about all this removal of God from our national life," Helen wrote to Welk on November 12, alluding to the Supreme Court decision to outlaw prayer in schools. ". . . I thought Thanksgiving was a wonderful time to remind everyone that this nation was <u>founded under God</u>." Welk agreed with her, and the poem was selected to be read on the Saturday before Thanksgiving, but fate intervened.

On Friday, November 22, President John F. Kennedy was assassinated in Dallas. Regular television programming was suspended while the networks covered the tragedy. Welk called Helen several times on Saturday, eventually reaching her at Gertrude's house in Lorain, where she had gone to spend the holiday and later appear at autograph shows. No less affected by the disaster than everyone else, he hoped to be able to honor the dead President. Could she, he asked, immediately write a tribute to John F. Kennedy that could be aired the following Saturday? She agreed without further discussion, and went to work that day. By Tuesday evening, Helen had completed two poems, which she sent via airmail to Welk. She left the choice up to him. Helen's "Tribute to J.F.K." was read by Aladdin on Saturday, November 30.

The response duplicated the "Praying Hands" phenomenon. An avalanche of requests for copies of the poem followed, with Gibson printing cards to supply its vendors and the Welk offices as well, and the stock diminishing faster than it could be replaced. Once again, Helen Steiner Rice had touched a nerve, and the effect was extraordinary. One woman wrote to her, describing the scene at a family gathering when the poem was read:

> Some of us were standing, some were sitting but we were all spellbound with the Truth, Beauty and Solemnity of it. We listened with awe; quietness reigned, and Mrs. Rice, when Aladdin finished we felt God was in our midst. No one spoke for minutes and I want to tell you, you will be forever blessed and taken care of for composing such a magnificent verse and proclaiming it to the world.

Her fame, however, exacted a price from Helen Steiner Rice. Everything now seemed to depend on the desires of a demanding public. As her popularity soared, so did the number of requests she received to make personal appearances and deliver speeches. To complicate matters, she found herself agreeing to write new booklets of poems at precisely the same time she vowed to answer as many fan letters as possible. Helen soon learned that she had

During the 1960s, people flocked to autograph shows to have Helen sign booklets of her poems. "To know her is to love her," wrote one fan.

imposed an impossible goal on herself. By January 1964, Helen realized that she was overwhelmed with obligations, so she decided to take steps that would make her schedule more reasonable. Her feelings were perhaps best expressed when she declined an invitation from Nora Wonning to speak in Batesville, Indiana:

> . . . the heart wants to do more than the hands are capable of. Right now I am about exhausted from trying to catalogue and answer Christmas fan mail. And while away on PERSONAL APPEARANCE TOURS my work pyramided mountain-high and I am hopelessly behind in my schedules. . . .
>
> We have had so many calls and letters recently in regard to speaking engagements that we have found it necessary to give everyone the same answer. After discussing this with our officers, we decided not to make any speaking commitments until we have formulated a more definite policy on the subject. . . .

While Helen regretted the loss of privacy, she steadfastly refused to let her new status interfere with commitments to her many friends. When she learned that her old friend and Gibson vice president, Jack Wiedemer, had injured his knee playing softball, Helen responded by writing a beautiful poem. Similarly, whenever someone at Gibson was celebrating a birthday, a retirement, or a job transfer, Helen could be counted on to "whip up" a verse for the occasion.

Helen also managed to find time for personal letters which helped others understand life's heartaches, offering profound advice dressed in simple words. Writing to a recently widowed mother of three children in February 1964, Helen recounted the death of her own father, construing it as a God-given "chance to grow in grace and soul stature":

> We often wonder why God chooses the darkness of sorrow as a path to Him but in the dazzling light of the day we cannot see beyond our own little world and living in the sunshine we become earthbound . . . but when the "darkness" comes our eyes are forced heavenward to the stars. For when it gets too dark for us to see our own hands then we must put our hand in the hand of GOD'S and let Him lead the way.

She also counseled a young man who was struggling with health problems, writing with kindness and conviction: "WHAT HAS HAPPENED IN YOUR LIFE cannot be solved by constantly wondering WHY???"

> If only we could "turn off our thoughts" . . . but John after years of battling this I have never conquered or curbed this endless sea of thoughts that comes unbidden, unsought and often unwelcome to break over my mind in wild confusion . . . but I have learned that all the thinking in the world does not change the conditions or the

circumstances or the situations I am daily confronted with . . . I CAN ONLY CHANGE MY ATTITUDE TOWARD THEM.

Trouble, Helen always believed, was a natural part of life that offered a chance to grow in faith and achieve inner peace. The increasing demands on her time presented Helen with ample opportunity to take her own advice. Reflecting on the problem, she freely admitted her own powerlessness:

> Right now I am hopelessly and helplessly entrapped and enmeshed and engulfed in conditions and situations that if I did not acknowledge my inability to change them I would break myself into pieces just trying!

Indeed, Helen found herself drowning more each day in the growing public demand for her inspirational works. Following a Gibson officers' meeting in July 1964, Bill Dresmann reported to Helen that her books had been discussed at great length, and that Fred Wagner was hoping Helen would soon find time to publish a hardcover book of all her inspirational poems. She was flattered by the compliment, but appalled at the prospect of taking on yet another assignment.

Wagner was not alone in his grasp of the scope of Helen's popularity. Bruce Forster, then general sales manager, wrote to Gibson dealers in September 1964: "Never before in the 114-year history of Gibson Greeting Cards has any merchandise received the 'tremendous' acclaim accorded Helen Steiner Rice's Inspirational Books." The sales impact of the reading of Helen's works on Lawrence Welk's show had been incredible, something Harry Hage noted in a *Gibson News Bulletin*: "This Inspirational Merchandise is the 'most successful' addition of new items to hit the greeting card market in many years if not in its history." By December 1964, a piece in the *New York Times* predicted that

Gibson's "Praying Hands" would be the top-selling Christmas card in the nation that year, with anticipated sales totaling 1.6 million copies.

Helen Steiner Rice's inspirational verses worked because they were able to "capture the hearts of people everywhere," to borrow the words of Louise Bacon, an industrial nurse at Gibson. In her own tribute, Nurse Bacon summarized the feelings of so many:

> To know Mrs. Rice is to love her. She is truly a thing of beauty in every sense of the word, physically, mentally and spiritually. One sees in her a radiance of The Gallilean portrayed so unmistakably vivid and the warmth of this Inner Being so seldom seen in humans today is so great you just have to be a better person. It's the greatest blessing I've ever had to be associated with her in the smallest way. She has been such an inspiration to me and has greatly influenced my Christian life more than she'll ever know.

In a nation torn by racial strife, anti-war demonstrations, and cultural upheaval, thousands of people saw in Helen Steiner Rice a ray of hope and goodness. New ways to showcase Helen's writings continually appeared: In 1964, a record album featuring Aladdin reading Helen's inspirational work was released by DOT records, and the next year Gibson Greetings sponsored a series of programs on the nationally broadcast "Don McNeill Breakfast Club" that brought readings of Mrs. Rice's work to all 315 stations of the ABC radio network every Wednesday morning. Helen Steiner Rice had taken the country by storm, and she did her best to react responsibly when approached by the hordes of people, professionals and amateurs alike, who hoped to work with her on literary and musical projects.

Most of the supplicants Helen could courteously dismiss, but others merited serious consideration. Foremost in the latter group was Jimmie Davis, the former governor of Louisiana and lyricist of "You Are My Sunshine," who called Helen in March 1965. A well-known gospel singer, Governor Davis was equally as prominent as Helen Steiner Rice and well connected with Decca records. At first, Helen was a bit skeptical about Davis's suggestion, made during a forty-five minute call, that they work together on inspirational recordings, but she did not reject his overture. Instead, Helen wrote to Lawrence Welk's secretary, Lois Lamont, mostly because Mr. Davis indicated that he knew Welk. Helen told Lois: "He says he is an ardent fan and has read all my books, and gives them away lavishly, and it occurred to him that they would go well on an inspirational record???"

Lois Lamont passed the letter along to Lawrence Welk himself, for he soon wrote back to Helen, who had been telling all promoters that she had an "unwritten allegiance" to Welk:

> Generally speaking, poems are usually not ideally suited for lyrics for songs, however, I would think that you would like to pursue some of your inquiries, especially the professional ones. It could conceivably be that a man like Jimmie Davis could use some of your material in an album very successfully.

Welk vouched for Davis as "a high-class gentleman in every respect," and counseled Helen that use of her material by Davis "would again hit an entirely new audience for you."

Reassured, Helen adopted a receptive attitude to suggestions Davis made in subsequent conversations. By May 1965, she was comfortable enough with Jimmie Davis's intentions to tell him about her "willingness to put my verses into your capable hands, subject to your talented treatment." She sensed no particular urgency about the project, however, and wrote Davis a verse expressing how she felt:

WHERE you'll begin
and WHAT you'll do . . .

No one knows
but GOD and YOU!
And I think right now
the answer is known
<u>NOT</u> to <u>YOU</u>
but to GOD ALONE . . .
So let's shove "it" back
away from the PRESENT
As something to THINK OF
that's TEMPTINGLY pleasant,
AND SOMETIME IN THE FUTURE
<u>if GOD wants "IT" TO BE</u>
He'll show you the door
and give you the key
And suddenly out of
the bright blue sky
You'll come up with a RECORD
that will hit a new high!

Heartened by her reaction, Jimmie Davis sent Helen several of his records, and she eagerly joined the ranks of his avid fans. She saw in his music a reflection of her own efforts to put spiritual truths into easily understandable words, and she fell in love with what she called "Davis' uncomplicated communicating with the heart." She wrote a stanza describing her inner joy to Lawrence Welk's secretary:

HOW MANY DOORS GOD OPENS
  FOR ME
AND SOMEHOW THEY ALWAYS
  HAPPEN TO BE

DOORS TO HEARTS THAT ARE
MUCH LIKE MY OWN
WHERE I FEEL "AT HOME" and
NEVER UNKNOWN.

Helen apparently believed she had found a soul mate in Jimmie Davis. She marveled that his gospel songs interpreted biblical thoughts in the same way she did. "You give me the feeling that you are not trying to PUT ON A PERFORMANCE," she wrote in July 1965, "but like me, you are DEDICATED and DEVOTED to 'SPREADING THE GREAT STORY.'"

Encouraged by her belief that she and Jimmie Davis shared a mission, Helen began to urge her fans to buy Davis's "soul-stirring" album *At the Crossing*. Her reason for doing so was simple; as she put it, the songs provided a "shelter for my heart." In fact, any schoolgirl listening to the music of her favorite rock star could not have been more enthusiastic than Helen was about the tunes of Jimmie Davis! She believed with all her heart that she had discovered a kindred spirit to help her explore the divine message to which she had devoted her life. With each successive letter and long-distance call, Helen became more willing to invest in their friendship and proposed enterprises.

It seems clear that Helen longed for affirmation from Jimmie Davis in what she believed was their joint mission. When it was not forthcoming, she reconsidered her need for his approval. Using the title from one of Governor Davis's gospel songs, "He Knows What I Need," Helen added the words "You Know Too," and wrote a private poem about how she had matured because of this disappointment:

Helen
Steiner Rice
Ambassador
of Sunshine

I asked for your Praise
You gave me none—

I asked for applause
and the words well done—
I ask for your plaudits,
Your Attention and Praise
Your "flowers of friendship"
Your sweet word Bouquets—
I ask for your "Love"
But you answered me not
I was terribly deflated
For I'd counted a lot
On having you like me
And admire me, too—
And tell me and tell me
What I meant to you—
But after I'd wept
And searched my "own heart"
I knew I'd been wrong
Right from the Start
I knew I was "older"
But still just a "Kid"
Demanding Attention
For All that I Did
So I've listened each day—
As you talked in Sweet Song
And patiently showed me
Where I had been Wrong—
Yes, You Know What I Need
And maybe some Day
Like Jesus you'll too
Wipe my tears all away.

219

To

Spread

"The

Great

Story"

Though they had never met, Helen felt she could depend on Governor Davis. In November 1965, when she learned that Doubleday and Company had approached Gibson about publishing a hardcover edition of her poems, the first thing Helen did was alert Jimmie Davis to the proposal. While Bill Dresmann went to New York to discuss the matter, Helen fretted that such an enterprise would somehow prevent others from using her verses. Moreover, she worried that if Doubleday copyrighted certain poems, it might limit her own use of them if she and Davis decided to collaborate on a musical project. As soon as he received her letter, the former governor called Helen, shrewdly recommending that she insist on an arrangement with Doubleday that satisfied her.

The Doubleday issue could not have come at a worse time. Helen already felt pressured to the breaking point, and to make matters worse, she had mysteriously developed "writer's block." To James Parr, pastor of Christ Methodist Church in Lorain, who was himself an aspiring poet, Helen poured out her frustration:

I have felt as dry and empty as an old wasp's nest . . . with not an idea in my mind . . . I am as barren as a mountain above timberline . . . and as unfertile as a fallow field . . . and like a frozen stream caught in the tight grip of winter. These "WINTERS OF THE MIND" are sheer torture and especially when you have SO MUCH TO DO.

While the Doubleday project percolated, Helen distracted herself as much as possible with professional concerns. She was scheduled for autograph shows in northern Ohio toward the end of November, and then shortly thereafter for three personal appearances in Atlanta. But even the travel had a raw edge. Perhaps it was a combination of overwork and stress, maybe even some lingering irritation with the way Gibson was handling the Doubleday proposal, but Helen eventually erupted in anger at a schedule that had her appearing in three locations during one afternoon.

"WHAT DO YOU THINK I AM???" the sixty-five-year-old lady wrote. "THIS IS NOT A MARATHON??? . . . I suppose I should get a SKATE BOARD to rush from place to place??? . . . YOU NOT ONLY WANT A POUND OF FLESH YOU DEMAND THE WHOLE BODY, MIND, SOUL, HEART and CADAVER as WELL!"

It was a weary Helen who went to Lorain for a Thanksgiving rest. Just before leaving Cincinnati, she wrote to a friend:

> Well, dear, it is very late and I am very tired and my heart is heavy . . . if I did not know that God never sends the Winter without following it by Spring and if I did not know that the darkest night ends in a sunrise I would think that God had forsaken or forgotten me. But surely in this tangled skein of my life I must soon come to the smooth, unknotted part.

Her fans, of course, had no inkling of how discouraged Helen felt, so her publicity appearances in northern Ohio were successful beyond measure. They produced feature stories and photographs in several newspapers, and Helen was especially gratified to see old friends who lined up in department stores to have her sign books for them. When she flew back to Cincinnati from Cleveland, Helen expected to change, pack another bag, and leave for Atlanta, where she was scheduled to introduce her newest softcover booklet, "LET NOT YOUR HEART BE TROUBLED." Things did not go as she intended, for as Helen later wrote, "God had other plans." Heart problems (attributed to overwork and exhaustion) suddenly brought her journey to an unexpected halt in Cincinnati. Her autograph shows and all other holiday plans were canceled so she could spend December recuperating. "Mother Nature" and "Father Time" combined to "clip my wings," she wrote, adding, "I know that GOD NEVER MAKES ANY MISTAKES. They say on the wings of GREAT DISAPPOINTMENTS come GREAT

COMPENSATIONS and I am sure that if I am patient God will reveal them to me."

Rested but still beleaguered at the beginning of the new year in 1966, Helen once again confronted the issue of the Doubleday proposal for a book of her poems. She obtained assurances from the editor, Sally Arteseros, that Helen's rights to use her own verses would not be compromised by the project. Negotiations with Gibson, however, proved more difficult. The letter of agreement drawn up by Gibson required Helen to concede that the poems had been written by her "as our employee." Since she had consistently maintained that her inspirational poems were written at home, not as part of her job as Gibson's editor, the assertion understandably rankled Helen. To make matters worse, Gibson wanted the right to contract with others for publication of a second book. Helen refused to sign. Gibson then balked at her counter-proposal, which limited the contract to a single volume of poems and allowed them to bid for her writings after Helen retired. In the spring of 1966, Bill Dresmann notified Doubleday that his company intended to abandon the project. He was crestfallen.

Bill Dresmann and Helen Steiner Rice had worked together for more than thirty years "in perfect unison," and had maintained what Helen called a "shiny-bright" friendship. In the aftermath of the Doubleday contract debacle, they conferred several times during the month of June. By July, enough progress had been made for Mr. Dresmann to report to Sally Arteseros that the "slight misunderstanding" between Helen and Gibson had been worked out. Thanks mostly to the goodwill that had long been established between Helen and Bill Dresmann, plans for publication of her first hardcover book of inspirational poems, *Just for You*, proceeded.

In August 1966, Helen wrote to Arteseros "off the record," explaining her version of the problems with Gibson that had stalled the project. According to her, much of the difficulty stemmed from dealing with C.I.T. Financial, the company that had acquired Gibson Greetings in 1964. Her carefully chosen words reveal how difficult it was for Helen to understand the changes beyond her control: "I am finding it daily a little more 'abrasive' to 'rub shoulders' with 'the strange impersonal monster' C.I.T. created out of our 'family circle.'" She ended by confiding that she only remained at Gibson because of Bill Dresmann and "a few other very nice people I have worked with for years." Helen also let Sally know that she would take a firm stance on future publications:

> But if Doubleday should ever conceive any more ideas of publishing Rice Books . . . do not contact Gibson for this is the <u>LAST THING I INTEND TO GIVE THEM</u>. . . . I do not mind sharing THE JEWELS GOD loaned me or GIVING THEM AWAY . . . if those who receive them appreciate their spiritual beauty and meaningfulness but it is foolish "to throw pearls to the swine."

While Helen struggled with Gibson—or more accurately, C.I.T. Financial—the ranks of those who appreciated her writing grew steadily. Many who wanted copies of her verses were young men assigned to duty in Vietnam, so Helen decided to author a special booklet of poems for servicemen, which she called "For Those In The Service Of Their Country." After several of the poems were brought to the attention of Lieutenant General Lewis B. Hershey, director of selective service, by Colonel Everette Stephenson of Kentucky, General Hershey wrote to Helen requesting a copy. Grateful that someone of Helen Steiner Rice's stature would devote so much time and effort to supporting the troops in Southeast Asia, he wanted to make sure she knew her work was appreciated.

As if things weren't complicated enough for Helen in the mid-1960s as she squabbled with Gibson and composed new inspirational poems, she also tried to make some sense of her relationship with Jimmie Davis. Helen had remained in close contact with

Louisiana's former governor for quite a while by this time, but by the summer of 1966, things changed. Davis told Helen that he planned to visit her in Cincinnati in August, and she was naturally excited at the prospect. Her eagerness to meet a person she called "the man of mystery" resembled the excitement of a teenager waiting for her first prom date. Everything seemed fine when Governor Davis arrived and they first met, but afterward Helen felt that he was more interested in becoming her manager than in artistic collaboration. Their plans to work together on a project quickly withered.

Whether or not her suspicions of Davis's motives were justified, Helen certainly had no need for a manager to help in boosting the sales of her verses. By the end of 1966, she was internationally recognized, for her writings had been translated into Afrikaans, they were being read on public buses in Hong Kong, and they were also being used in Bible classes in Japan and India. Helen's popularity in the United States was even greater than it was abroad, and it steadily increased. Her cards, booklets, and framed poems were snapped up as fast as they appeared on distributors' shelves, and in the last months of 1966, dealers eagerly anticipated the holiday season by purchasing more than 200,000 calendars featuring Helen's writings. When Ernest Rice wrote to his "dear little Jingle Belle" in December 1966, congratulating his aunt on her many successes, he had no idea that she had only arrived at a threshold in her career. Beyond it was the promise of reaching even greater audiences. The publication of her first hardcover book, due for release early in 1967, proved to be the key.

8

*Like a
Flower
in the
Sun*

elen readily admitted that she found her own popularity overwhelming. In an interview that coincided with the March 1967 release of her book, she told a *Cincinnati Enquirer* reporter: "I'm very happy that I can give something through my poetry, but it is frightening because people have a tendency to endow you with attributes you can't possibly have." She also raised the issue of her new status and how she should deal with it in a conversation with long-time friend Jack Wiedemer. She showed him a letter from a lady who was convinced that if Helen came to visit her church, the church would then be blessed. "Jack," she said, "you know that isn't true, and I know that isn't true, but if she thinks that's true I guess that's still good." Helen worried less about fame than about whether her work was doing any good. If it was, nothing else mattered.

The international acclaim of Helen's verses made the success of her Doubleday book a foregone conclusion. Nevertheless, everyone involved in the project at Gibson Greetings prepared carefully for the March 24, 1967, publication date. Some even went so far as to describe the event as "one of the most important announcements in Gibson's 117-year history." The slender volume, entitled *Just for You*, was only sixty-four pages from beginning to end, but

The publication in 1967 of Helen's first hardcover book, Just for You, *thrilled her long-time friend, Gibson vice president Bill Dresmann.*

the book's brevity was more than offset by its content. The cover featured Albrecht Dürer's "Praying Hands," and Helen's poem of the same name was the centerpiece of the collection. Gently scolding the company for what she viewed as corporate greed, Helen arranged for her share of the advance royalty check to be divided between Christ Methodist Church in Lorain and Wesley Chapel in Cincinnati. Helen's public did not, of course, know anything about royalty arrangements; they simply bought the book wherever they could find it. Within a few days of its release, Gibson's copies of the book had completely sold out. By June, Doubleday had shipped sixty-seven thousand additional copies of *Just for You* to Gibson for distribution, and had sold seventeen thousand more through its own outlets.

Her fame made Helen's life a nightmare, with scarcely enough time to breathe. She found herself constantly besieged by requests

Helen's appearance before the Lakeland Women's Club of Lorain in November 1967 was a triumphant homecoming.

Helen
Steiner Rice
*Ambassador
of Sunshine*

to give speeches, publish books, write more poems, and help individuals in need—all while earning her salary at Gibson Greetings. She described her days as "pressure-packed and tension-torn," and often lamented: "my days are over and done before I have even half begun to do the things I want to do." Years earlier, Helen had cut back on speaking engagements in an effort to reserve some time for her writing. Yet, every once in a while, she recalled the thrill of electrifying an audience, so she occasionally made exceptions to her rule. One notable occasion was when she accepted an invitation to address the Lakeland Women's Club of Lorain in November 1967.

No one could have received a warmer greeting that autumn than Helen did when she stood before the women who packed Christ Methodist Church to hear her inspirational message. As she looked out at the crowd, Helen saw childhood friends who had known her as a playmate or classmate. Now they were women, most of them with families, and all with cares that only they knew. Humbled by the opportunity to speak to them, Helen's message came straight from the heart: "You recognize what's inside of you by your interpretation of what I write." Helen's talk moved her audience, and the reporters who attended the affair gave it headline coverage in the women's sections of local newspapers. Helen's attire also attracted attention, particularly her hat. The women's editor of the *Lorain Journal* provided a detailed account of it as a turban of silver and green brocade that complemented her kellygreen silk suit, matching shoes, and long, silver gloves.

Impressed though Helen's friends may have been by her visit, she likened the experience of speaking in her hometown to the Spanish Inquisition. Relieved once it was behind her, Helen reported to Doubleday's Sally Arteseros that it "turned out to be quite a nice tribute to me. . . . I am told they had an all time high attendance even though the day was utterly miserable with rain coming down in torrents." She was fond of Sally, but when the young editor urged her to do another book of poems for Doubleday, Helen replied with an emphatic "no."

The publisher was naturally interested in developing new projects with Helen Steiner Rice, but Doubleday was not the only company eager to offer Helen's messages of hope and perseverance to the public. Several other publishing houses had also contacted her, foremost among them the Fleming H. Revell Company. Their proposal especially intrigued Helen because they offered to publish a biographical essay as an introduction to her next verse collection.

From Helen's perspective, there was much to be said for switching to a new publisher. She wished to avoid the pain that came with Doubleday's apparent preference for dealing with Gibson rather than with her, and more importantly, the people at Revell seemed attuned to what she was trying to accomplish—she felt they understood and supported her inspirational ministry. Besides,

Helen felt utterly betrayed by the contract Gibson had forged with Doubleday, and opened her heart to James Parr, her former pastor in Lorain, when she bitterly wrote:

> I just received my second royalty check, which is small compared to what it should be . . . for Gibson pays me nothing for the 67,000 books they sold. They use this to pay the salesmen their commission, and for their own margin of profit. Then they "un-abashedly" take half of what DOUBLEDAY sends me for their sales.

In the end, Helen decided to leave Doubleday and cast her lot with Revell.

By February 1968, Helen had made arrangements with the Fleming H. Revell Company to publish a book that included poems and a biographical sketch. The next month, Revell's associate editor, Donald Kauffman, visited Helen in Cincinnati to discuss the biographical portion of the book, tentatively entitled *Heart Gifts*. Within a few weeks, by April 1968, the manuscript had been sent to Revell, edited, and then returned to Helen for her approval. Since she liked Kauffman, Helen felt an obligation to correct and return the materials quickly, but there were just too many claims on her time; she missed the deadline, and wrote apologetically to Mr. Kauffman:

Oh how I wish I had wings on my heels, a song in my heart, and magic in my hands, so that with a swish of the wrist I could give this

Helen believed that she and her many fans formed a "human chain of love" around the world.

Like a Flower in the Sun

all the "fairy-tale treatment" by waving my wand . . . and instantly everything would be ALL RIGHT and everybody would be HAPPY. . . .

Unsatisfied with that explanation, she added another, quipping in verse that it would be much simpler:

> *If only YOU WERE HERE*
> *Or I WAS THERE . . .*
> *We'd have NO TROUBLE then,*
> *For I can use "my little tongue"*
> *MUCH FASTER than "MY PEN"???*

In fact, the demands on Helen had become so great by this time that she was relying heavily on her secretary, Mary Jo Eling, to help her wade through requests, answer correspondence, and meet deadlines. Miss Eling had been with Helen for less than a year when she praised Mary Jo to Kauffman without qualification, writing: "She is the only ray of sunshine on my 'dark horizon' right now . . . she is about the nicest thing that came into my life." Until the end of Helen's life, she referred to her secretary as "the incomparable Mary Jo."

Simply dealing with the volume of fan mail that came into Helen's office was a staggering task, even with help from Mary Jo, for thousands of letters poured in from all over the world. Still, Helen managed to compose a personal answer to most of them because in her mind, her admirers formed a human network stretching around the globe and working in her behalf to spread "The Great Story."

Helen's files overflowed with letters from people who had never met her but still kept up a correspondence over the years because they sensed her concern and felt transformed by it. A woman in Michigan, for example, wrote: "I feel impelled to let you know how God has met me and fed my hungry soul and sick body with the ministry of your poems." Another fan responded to Helen's words of encouragement in a letter that concluded: "I felt the warm glow of your sincere and radiant personality and realize that you know God. . . ." Upon receiving a package from Helen, another of her correspondents studied her picture and wrote: "You are just as beautiful inside as you are outside, like a precious gem, yes, a diamond. You always glitter from the inside out. . . ."

Often, Helen affected other people's lives profoundly when a particular poem crossed their path at exactly the right moment. On one occasion, a woman in Albuquerque, New Mexico, was recovering from cancer. Embittered by the indifference of her husband and feeling very lonely, she went from one church to another, searching for comfort that never came. Just when she reached the brink of despair, a friend sent her a card that included Helen's poem, "God Knows Best." It affected her in an indescribable way, far beyond anything she had experienced before. Inspired, she began her own ministry, compassionately reaching out to others and sending them copies of the verse that had changed her life. When she reported what happened, Helen responded: "I can see from your letter that you are 'giving yourself away,' and nothing enriches us so much as when we do that. For we become so engrossed in doing for others that we completely forget about our own trouble."

Another of Helen's verses changed the life of Kathleen Mimms, a Sunday school teacher in Newport, Kentucky, who first wrote to Helen in March 1968. Miss Mimms simply wanted to let Helen know that her poem, "The End of the Road is But a Bend in the Road," had kept her from despair and self-destruction as she dealt with leukemia. Seeing in Kathleen that same loneliness she herself often experienced, Helen soon developed both an affection for her and a deep admiration for the courage she showed while contending with the frequent hospitalizations and surgeries caused by the cancer spreading through her body. In letter after letter, Helen encouraged Kathleen to draw on an awareness of God's love to cope with her physical trials.

By July 1970, when the malignancy had spread to Miss Mimms's face, requiring the removal of her left jawbone and all her teeth, she wrote to Helen that no matter what happened, she was determined to lead her Bible classes again by the end of the summer. Kathleen summed up her feelings by remarking: "Who cares about a lop-sided face—I can't even smile now but I am smiling inside—I can still touch and feel and love. And next to God, Mrs. Rice, I love you because without you none of this could have been. God understands how I feel about you—He sent you to me."

Helen was naturally affected by Kathleen's sentiments, but she was reluctant to write a somber reply to someone undergoing such a terrible ordeal. Instead, she responded with a combination of lighthearted verse and spiritual counsel drawn from the depths of personal experience.

> *Dear "WONDER GIRL,"*
> *You're a MARVEL and a MIRACLE . . .*
> *you're LOVELY and you're LYRICAL . . .*
> *you're BEAUTIFUL inside and out . . .*
> *and, most of all, there is no doubt . . .*
> *you SYMBOLIZE what "AN ANGEL"*
> *should be . . .*
> *and you're TRULY AN INSPIRATION to*
> *ME! . . .*

My dear, I know all that you endured. But somehow the GLOW of GOD'S NEARNESS to YOU filtered through the whole letter, and it completely OVERBALANCED EVERY-THING, and I felt you had experienced what so few people do.

My dear, you have such close rapport with GOD that even during "THE DARKEST HOURS" you are able to walk in "THE LIGHT" . . . and that is something only "THE CHOSEN" ever know anything about!

Kathleen Mimms had been given less than two years to live in 1968, when she began her correspondence with Helen. The mutually beneficial connection between the two women spanned nearly thirteen years, with Miss Mimms continually encouraged in her struggle against a ravaging disease by Helen's support.

An equally affirming experience for Helen came when she struck up a friendship with Stella Bright Ullom, an elderly shut-in living in a Pittsburgh housing project, who began writing to Helen in September 1968. Like Kathleen Mimms, Stella Ullom was convinced that Helen's poems had the power to work miracles. From the beginning, Stella felt a certain comfort in sharing everything that was precious to her with Helen. On one occasion Stella related the tale of her niece's son, who had been killed in a train accident ten years earlier. The boy's mother had neither cried nor spoken of him after the funeral, but when she and Miss Ullom next met, Stella showed the grieving mother several letters and cards sent by Helen. Stella reported to Mrs. Rice:

> She read the sympathy cards and all of a sudden she laid her head on the table and sobbed uncontrollably. GOD THROUGH YOU HAD OPENED THE FLOOD GATES AND ALL THE ANGUISH THAT HAS BEEN STORED IN HER HEART FOR TEN YEARS WAS POURED OUT IN ALMOST INCOHERENT WORDS AND BROKEN SENTENCES.
>
> After she had regained control of herself, she thanked me for letting her see and read your poems and told me they were the FIRST THINGS THAT HAD REALLY TOUCHED HER SINCE SHE HEARD THE NEWS OF THE TRAGEDY! THEN SHE TALKED ABOUT DONNIE, AND ABOUT GOD! . . .

When she bade me "Good-bye" she said: "<u>I SHALL PRAY FOR HELEN STEINER RICE!</u> TELL HER THAT ONLY <u>HER</u> POEMS HAVE EVER BEEN ABLE TO <u>REACH MY HEART!</u> TELL HER ALSO THAT MY FOUNTAIN OF TEARS WAS DRY, OR SO I THOUGHT, UNTIL SHE OPENED THE FLOOD GATES!"

Later, Stella, who had been christened "Star Bright" by Helen, attributed a dramatic change in her own life to her correspondent. Stella confided to Helen a terrible secret from her youth. As a young girl in The Salvation Army, she had been sexually molested by a male officer. To make matters worse, when Stella told her story to female officers, they beat her and demanded that she withdraw her charges. Stella did so rather than bring shame to the offending officer's "good family." Ever afterward, she was branded a liar and treated as a pariah by many members of The Salvation Army. To her credit, Stella rose above the unfairness of an ordeal that would test anyone's soul. Her sin, she told Helen, was not so much hating those who betrayed her, but rather letting that hate blot from her sight any sense of her own worth. Helen's constant affirmation of Stella's value—despite her ordeal, her frailties, and her failings—brought about a complete transformation in the old Salvation Army worker.

"DEAR BEAUTIFUL, BLESSED SAINT . . . ," Stella began one letter, "you have blessed my soul as no other human being ever has. . . . You have given me what I needed so much—appreciation." She concluded with: "I felt so unworthy—and you have rekindled my self-respect." Like so many others who sensed that Helen Steiner Rice had changed their lives, Stella Ullom wrote faithfully, on an almost-daily basis, to the woman who had opened up aspects of life that she had never imagined. Eventually, Stella thanked her benefactor with a poetic "Tribute to Helen Steiner Rice." It ended with a tender summary of what Helen's work meant to her:

*This gracious, Christian woman thus
    portrays the story of
God's plan for man's redemption and His
    OWN ineffable LOVE!*

Others were also affected by Helen's sentiments in very personal
ways. A lady from Illinois wrote to Helen, "Tonight I have read
your book entitled *Just for You.* I am ashamed but also happy to
admit that until one hour before the time of this writing I never
truly realized what life was. Life is God. God is Love. Love is Giving. . . . My only hope is that through me, others can feel the way
I do. You are truly God's 'agent.'" Letters like these left Helen
with mixed feelings. She felt honored to be able to help others;
but she felt an increasing sense of duty and urgency to use her
influence to bring about positive change in the world.

This sense of mission led Helen to approach Walter Holmes, Jr.,
executive vice president of Gibson's parent company, C.I.T. Financial, with a proposal for forging an alliance between the business
and creative sides of the corporation. Her argument was compelling, and Helen delivered it without obscuring rhetoric: "I feel
that our hearts must keep in step with our heads or we become
insensitive, unfeeling, and rich materially but poverty-stricken spiritually." Convinced that kindheartedness and success in big business were quite compatible, Helen did not believe that businessmen had to be steely-eyed, nor that creative artists needed to be
self-indulgent and irresponsible, so she issued a challenge to Mr.
Holmes:

Don't misunderstand me . . . I am all for competitive business. But
let us compete not only for being BIGGEST but the BEST. And to
be the BEST, we have to build not only an economical empire but
a KINGDOM of GOODNESS and JUSTICE. There are certainly
many frontiers that we have never explored, and the KINGDOM of

GOD is still an UNDISCOVERED CONTINENT. When we discover this continent . . . not in a narrow, churchy way but in a workable way . . . then nothing can ever defeat us . . . for there is enough of EVERYTHING in this world for EVERYBODY . . . and it is up to men of your stature to help work this out.

Ever more aware of her own charisma, Helen was determined to play a vital part in helping to build a kingdom of goodness. As always, fate stepped in to give her many opportunities to test her sense of purpose. In the spring of 1968, the Little Sisters of the Poor brought a group of elderly residents to Gibson for a tour. As soon as Helen learned about the visitors, she left her work to meet with them personally, and the seniors responded as enthusiastically to her warmth as the correspondents in New Mexico and Illinois who had never met her. "Old people are very sensitive to attention," Sister Louise wrote to Helen after the visit, "especially ours, since so many of them feel neglected by their own loved ones. . . . You were more than nice to them and you treated each one of them as ROYALTY! They are still talking about it to the envy of all the residents who were unable to make the trip."

In the late 1960s, just as in the 1920s, it seemed that whatever she did, Helen Steiner Rice was destined to be a major attraction. No sooner had the North American Christian Convention planned its July 1968 meeting for the Cincinnati Convention Center than its organizers asked Helen to address a special women's session of the conference. Unsure about what to do, Helen discussed the invitation with several Gibson executives she trusted. They all encouraged her to accept, noting that the gathering would draw fifteen thousand people engaged in Christian ministries. Moreover, her friends pointed out that the NACC used Helen's work on their radio broadcasts and in their publications. In the end, she was swayed by this advice and agreed to accept the invitation, mostly because she felt that she "really owed them a speech." It was the

238

Helen
Steiner Rice
Ambassador
of Sunshine

right decision, for when the time came on the morning of July 10, 1968, Helen Steiner Rice walked into a hall packed front-to-back and side-to-side with twenty-five hundred women—a "standing room only" crowd that took everyone by surprise. The audience was mesmerized as Helen talked from the heart about her faith in God, punctuating her comments by reading several of her poems.

Any doubts Helen felt about speaking to the assembly were erased, first when she saw the enormous crowd, and then when her talk received three standing ovations. She was simply over-whelmed. In the days following her appearance, letters poured in to Gibson's mail room from convention-goers who had been deeply moved by her message. It had a profound effect on Helen, who savored the occasion, describing it as "one of the most rewarding and enriching experiences of my entire life." She subse-quently wrote: "As I looked across that crowded, jam-packed room into the radiant faces of these 'BEAUTIFUL PEOPLE,' I knew they were truly clean and shiny-bright both INSIDE and OUT . . . and it put me in an 'upswept mood' for many days."

Helen Steiner Rice met hundreds of people during the 1968 meeting of the North American Christian Convention. But when she reflected on it, the most rewarding part of the experience was her meeting with May Hockley, the minister's wife who intro-duced her to that overflowing room at Cincinnati's Convention Center. Afterward, Helen developed and then maintained a friend-ship with Mrs. Hockley, who she called "one of the MOST CHARMING . . . CAPABLE . . . COMPETENT . . . and COM-PLETELY CAPTIVATING CHRISTIANS whom I have ever met." May Hockley, her husband, and their two daughters epito-mized the perfect Christian family to Helen. "We need MORE HOMES like THE HOCKLEY'S, where REAL LOVE STORIES are lived daily!" Helen later wrote in tribute to her friend.

In November 1968, Helen's second book, *Heart Gifts*, was published by Revell. She had already worked out an arrangement with them that mirrored the earlier agreement with Doubleday in which Helen signed her royalties over to churches in Lorain and Cincinnati. Her extraordinary record of giving made Helen Steiner Rice an obvious choice when, in December 1968, a Christ Methodist Church Committee unanimously selected her as the ideal spokesperson to address their Lorain congregation on the topic of "Why I Support My Church." "Money spent for GOD'S work is the BEST SPENT MONEY!" Helen explained in a note to her pastor, William Bullock. She also sent him a pithy little verse, which he published in the church bulletin:

It isn't WISE to ECONOMIZE
when SPENDING for THE LORD—
GIVE HIM HIS SHARE
and a little to SPARE
and GREAT will be your reward!

Meanwhile, fate dealt a blow to Wesley Chapel in Cincinnati that severely tested Helen's patience. She had faithfully attended services at the little Methodist church for nearly four decades, so Helen Steiner Rice was understandably upset when she learned that Cincinnati's premier company, Procter and Gamble, had acquired the property where Wesley Chapel stood and planned to raze the 175-year-old church. Procter and Gamble had gone more than the proverbial extra mile in working with Methodism's hierarchy to preserve the historic building—the company even offered to move the chapel to a new location—but the leadership of the church was adamant. They were determined to get rid of the old church and put their resources into creating a new ministry in the poverty-ridden Over-the-Rhine district of Cincinnati. If Helen had any knowledge of what was going on behind the scenes, she never expressed it. To her it was simple: Corporate executives and church administrators had missed the point. Helen believed that the demise of Wesley Chapel was nothing less than a catastrophe, one that left her angry and depressed.

In January 1969, she wrote to Wilbur Davies, chairman of Revell's executive committee, that the impending destruction of Wesley Chapel weighed heavily on her heart. "It is almost 175 years old, but PROCTER AND GAMBLE has been wanting to tear it down and enlarge their soap empire. So again the MATERIAL has triumphed over the SPIRITUAL with a few swift, crunching swings of the giant juggernaut." Helen included a poem, entitled "Current Comments," with her letter to Mr. Davies:

> *There was "NO ROOM in THE INN"*
> *when the Christ Child came,*
> *and after two thousand years*
> *things are still the same—*
> *For there still is NO ROOM*
> *for the CHURCH of CHRIST*
> *In face of an offer*
> *that is high enough priced,*
> *And there still is NO ROOM*
> *in the "HEART OF MAN"*
> *If God and the Church*
> *interfere with his plan—*
> *And the BISHOP agrees*
> *with the COMMERCIAL CZAR*
> *That logically speaking*
> *with things as they are*
> *It is ethically sound*
> *and good business, too,*
> *To condemn Wesley Chapel*
> *to the "GREAT WRECKING*
> *CREW"—*

For historic Wesley
now means nothing more
Than an outmoded building
there's no further use for,
And the GIANTS of BUSINESS
can boastfully say —
WHY PRAY when "OUR SOAP"
washes "ALL STAINS" away!

Obviously, nearly seventy years had not blunted the stinging wit that Helen Steiner Rice had employed in political satire for decades. Wesley Chapel became a symbol of what always vexed Helen the most—a feeling of powerlessness to effect change. A sense of inadequacy overwhelmed her as she read the continuous stream of letters that flooded her office. She confided her frustration to Wilbur Davies:

> It is impossible to read through this daily fan mail and go unscathed and untouched by the tragic things that are happening in the lives of more people than we even dare to allow ourselves to think about. And that in itself is a great tragedy. We try to push these unhappy things away from us so that our own lives are not too darkened by the shadows all around us.

Helen's self-assessment, born of doubt and despair, was, of course, inaccurate, for there had never been a time when she turned her back on the heartache of others. It was, in fact, her willingness to embrace the pain of friends and strangers alike that brought about what they saw as "miracles" in their lives.

For those like Stella Ullom, Kathleen Mimms, and countless others who depended on her sustaining letters and verses, Helen Steiner Rice always seemed to have kindness and compassion to spare. Any listing of her daily routine bespeaks boundless energy and determination to spread the "good news of God's love."

Helen
Steiner Rice
Ambassador
of Sunshine

Always modest to a fault, Helen was nevertheless aware of the cost of her devotion to duty. Once, when she was asked about taking vacations, Helen answered with a little verse:

> *PLANNED VACATIONS are a LUXURY*
>   *I no longer indulge in!*
> *I'm entitled to each MONDAY OFF*
> *and the MAXIMUM VACATION . . .*
>   *But when I'm in "THE MIDST OF*
>   *WORK,"*
> *like "directors on location,"*
>   *I can't afford to "drop it all,"*
> *nor would I care to try . . .*
>   *I'd rather go vacationing*
> *when <u>MY MIND is DULL and DRY</u>!*

As Helen entered her seventies she could feel the refining hand of God at work in all areas of her life. It was a trying time of emotional turbulence worsened by physical limitation. In January 1970, Helen cautiously revealed the extent of her pain to the Gradisons when she wrote, "Dottie dear, I could not have put it into better words than you did when you said . . . 'At this point, I don't really believe I can be of much help to anyone—even myself!' . . . for that is exactly the way I feel." Helen could find no relief from a growing number of aches and pains, and she had been constantly frustrated by receptionists when she tried to see her doctors over the holiday season. "To die is very easy, but to live is really a problem!" she exclaimed. "I have just discovered there is no one you can really count on in this world except GOD. HE is never too busy to listen to you. HE never tells you to come back another time. And when you need HIM, you know HE is right there!"

Sometimes, Helen had days when everything seemed to go wrong. In the spring of 1970, she was in a frenzy trying to complete another book for the Fleming H. Revell Company. Upset by various pressures, Helen took out her discontent on Phyllis Murphy, Revell's managing editor, in a stinging critique of her revisions of the manuscript. Then, scarcely missing a beat, she apologized in verse for magnifying "little mistakes."

> *If I sounded "UPTIGHT" and*
>   *FRAZZLED and FRAYED,*
> *DEPLETED, DISCOURAGED,*
>   *DERANGED and DISMAYED,*
> *I sounded EXACTLY THE WAY I WAS*
>   *FEELING*
> *With a MIXED, MUDDLED MIND and*
>   *a HEAD that was REELING . . .*
> *SO SORRY you called "in the midst of the*
>   *storm"*
> *When "my world was all wet" and "blown*
>   *out of form" . . .*
> *sure hope our next "visit" IS ALL TO THE*
>   *GOOD*
> *WITH EVERYTHING GOING THE*
>   *WAY THAT IT SHOULD!*

The book at issue, *Lovingly,* proved to be one of Helen's most popular efforts. Published in October 1970, its success amazed Revell's executives and Helen as well. Her joy was diluted, however, by the sudden death of her friend, the Cincinnati "big band" leader Barney Rapp. Coming, as it did, during the month of October, when Helen was always melancholy because of Franklin Rice's sad death decades earlier, the loss of her old friend especially grieved Helen. Doing her best to cope with the situation, she wrote to Mary Jane Ross, a friend at Revell:

> Of course, I have experienced this feeling of "lost-loneliness" many times through the 38 years that Franklin has been gone, and it seems a mist of melancholia drifts in like a fog and there is nothing I can do until the fog lifts. But I know that "THIS, TOO, WILL PASS AWAY." However, each year it gets a little more difficult to struggle through the fog.

Still in a blue mood at the end of October, Helen lamented further to Mary Jane—who had become a confidant despite the fact that she was far away in New Jersey—that she was distraught because coworkers were being let go as Gibson streamlined its operations. With a sympathy born as much of her own pain as an understanding of the plight of others, Helen told Mary Jane: "They have been going over a list of people nearing the retirement age and cutting them down like FIELD GRASS before a MECHANI-CAL MOWER."

Mrs. Ross was not the only one to whom Helen unburdened herself. When Dorothy Gradison sent her a box of holiday treats in November, Helen responded with a thank-you note that expressed her feelings without equivocation: "Right now, I am so heartsick and so soul-saddened, [that] nothing but a closer walk with GOD could put a song in my heart." Helen did, however, send her love and friendship to Mrs. Gradison in a verse that underscored the values she had always held dear:

> *For stores don't sell a single thing*
> *To make the HEART that's troubled*
>   *SING . . .*
> *The joys of life that cheer and bless*
> *The stores don't sell, I must confess . . .*

But FRIENDS and PRAYERS are
*   "PRICELESS TREASURES"*
Beyond ALL MONETARY
*   MEASURES . . .*
and so I say a SPECIAL PRAYER
that GOD WILL KEEP YOU IN HIS
*   CARE . . .*
and if I can ever help you, dear,
in any way throughout the year,
You've only to call, for as long as I live
"SUCH AS I HAVE, I FREELY GIVE!"

By Christmas 1970, Helen's emotional woes were compounded by a physical handicap she believed to be arthritis, which became increasingly painful and less responsive to medication. "I am having a very difficult time," she wrote to Dorothy Gradison after the family had gone to Florida for the winter. At this time of her life, the departure of the Gradisons was more painful than Helen could describe, for she missed them so much. After all, Helen and Gertrude had spent many Christmases with the Gradison family. "It is going to seem very strange not to SHARE that ONE, LOVELY HOLIDAY with you," she wrote to Dorothy, adding that she would think of them as the celebration of Chanukah began. "We will just feel we are all TOGETHER, even though miles divide us," Helen concluded.

The physical pain Helen felt proved to be a harbinger of things to come, for repeated tests showed that arthritis was not the problem. Instead, it was much worse; the doctors told her that she was suffering from a deteriorating spinal condition, probably originating from a serious fall or infection that had occurred earlier in her life. Naturally, she was upset by the diagnosis, but her old spirit of meeting adversity head-on prevailed. In early February 1971, she made light of her problems, writing to the Gradisons that in spite

Helen
Steiner Rice
Ambassador
of Sunshine

of the disintegration of two discs in her back, the doctor had told her: "You have a very good heart, good lungs, and good blood, and you may live a long, long time." Putting the best possible face on her malady, she quipped: "So, Willis, I guess maybe you and I will get that WILL made out before I die after all!"

Helen found the limp that accompanied her spinal problems harder to accept than the pain. "I LOVED BEING FLEET OF FOOT," she wrote to Dot and Willis, "and I guess most females really do not want to look like 'THE LEANING TOWER OF PISA' or 'THE HUNCHBACK OF NOTRE DAME!'" Yet just as she mourned the loss of her physical powers, it was consistent with Helen's prayerful nature that she saw every event in her life as a call to a deeper spirituality. She tried to explain how she felt to the Gradisons when she wrote:

> In Psalm 119:71, it says, "IT IS GOOD FOR ME THAT I HAVE BEEN AFFLICTED," and I certainly am not going to argue with GOD on that score. . . . for no one can ever sway my thinking that GOD NEVER MAKES MISTAKES. I am sure "THIS" is just HIS METHOD of slowing me down and pushing me into semi-retirement. . . . So, I think my prayer should be, "DEAR GOD, HELP ME TO DISCRIMINATE BETWEEN A 'SHATTERED EGO' AND A 'SHATTERED SPINE'!"

As it turned out, Helen was not alone in her suffering. Dorothy Gradison responded to her letter in March, reporting that she, too, had been so plagued by health problems that they had forced her to become a "woman of few words." Helen immediately sympathized, and encouraged Dorothy to conserve her energy. Always trying to make the most of a trying situation, Helen drew on her personal experience to comfort her friend:

> I can say that I am "LIMPING ALONG with MORE AGILITY" these days. I think after you adjust to your problem and realize you have annexed it for life, you start trying to capitalize on it. So, I just

"LIMP ALONG a LITTLE SLOWER," and it is a perfect excuse for not being forever in "HIGH GEAR" or travelling at "HIGH SPEED!"

She then kidded Dorothy about Willis's "new look"—that of a stockbroker who bowed to the current fashion in facial hair—which Helen had observed when Mr. Gradison stopped to help her fill out her tax forms:

IMAGINE MY ASTONISHMENT! IMAGINE MY SURPRISE! TO FIND "OUR ULTRA CONSERVATIVE" was a "HIPPIE in DISGUISE!" I can't tell you how absolutely overcome I was to open the door and see this HANDSOME, HIRSUTE HIPPIE with a MOD MUSTACHIO and MINIATURE SIDEBURNS . . . which goes to show that these ULTRA CONSERVATIVE PEOPLE are really REACTIONARY REBELS!

Of all the ordeals that marked the stages of her declining years—physical disabilities, spiritual crises, and a general feeling that she had lost control of her own life—Helen was most overwhelmed by tax problems. They held an unexplainable, unspeakable terror for Helen, so it was vitally important that Willis Gradison, who had been her trusted financial advisor throughout most of her adult life, guide her as she waded through Internal Revenue Service forms that grew more complex with each passing year. "I sure will breathe a sigh of relief when the forms are typed and on their way to 'THE REVENUE ROBBERS' . . . ," she confessed to Dot, "and 'ROBBERS' they are, for they make JESSE JAMES look like a RANK AMATEUR!" The decisions Helen had to make about her taxes were insignificant, however, when compared to the career choices she made as she neared her seventy-first birthday.

In 1971, after nearly forty years of loyal service, Helen officially retired as editor at Gibson. Instead of severing her connection to the company completely, she remained affiliated with Gibson as a consultant and retained an office there. The new arrangement enabled Helen to continue to work with Mary Jo Eling in answering the steady stream of correspondence that flowed in from across the country and around the world. This transition was emotionally difficult for Helen, and she explained it to long-time confidant Audrey Carroll: "I am still coming into my office. I am on a retired basis, but I come in daily, because I am working for GOD and not for GIBSON! And while I am ready and wanting to go, I am willing to stay as long as GOD has work for me to do, for this is my complete JOY and HAPPINESS."

Ironically, just at the time when age and circumstances dictated that Helen must retire, she was reaching more people than ever before. Her books sold thousands of copies each year, and her admirers could not get enough of her wit and wisdom. Considering her popularity, it was natural for Revell to suggest that Helen compile another volume of her verses to satisfy the public's demand. Since Helen was happy with the way Revell had treated her, she began work on a new book, tentatively entitled *Prayerfully,* early in 1971. Enthusiastic about the project, she wrote to Mary Jane Ross that the title of the book alone had been enough to trigger "all kinds of new ideas."

It was not by accident that Helen first told Mary Jane Ross about this new project, for she was especially fond of Mary Jane and valued her opinion. A tribute she penned about her friend that August of 1971 was more than praise for a confidant; it was also a revealing self-portrait:

You've seen me "under pressure" . . . and you've heard me RANT and RAVE . . . and yet you're RIGHT BEHIND ME . . . when I KID-LIKE MISBEHAVE??? . . . No wonder I ADMIRE YOU . . . and THINK YOU'RE QUITE A GIRL . . . for in my "FRIENDSHIP JEWEL CASE" . . . YOU ARE A RARE AND PRICELESS PEARL!

But I'd like to be "LESS VOLATILE" . . . and "MORE QUI-
ETLY COMPOSED" . . . but it seems my ACTIVE NERVE
ENDS . . . are all SHATTERED and EXPOSED . . . and I POP
OFF LIKE A PISTOL . . . that is ready to be fired . . . and folks like
that . . . are JUST THE TYPE that I NEVER HAVE ADMIRED.
. . . No wonder I am BAFFLED and AWED with WONDER, too
. . . that GOD keeps on FORGIVING ME, and SO DO FOLKS
LIKE YOU!

Forgiveness was still very much on Helen's mind when, nearly a
month later, on September 5, 1971, she thought about her long-
dead husband. Franklin's last birthday was on that date in 1932,
and recalling it brought a flood of memories. During the four
decades since he had died, Helen had repeatedly asked God to
help her understand the purpose of Franklin's death. Finally, she
felt she had an answer, and she wrote to Audrey Carroll:

I feel he [Franklin] sacrificed his life that the end of my life might
be lived in a fuller and richer way. When he went away so suddenly,
he transformed my entire life, for I never could have done all this
on my own nor could I have felt the things I feel so deeply. That is
why, in some way which is unfathomable to me, it is Franklin who
has contributed so much to my life, and he did it not in LIVING
but in dying.

Reminiscences of Franklin's tragic and early death, as well as
that of her father (both occurred in October), combined to plunge
Helen into a seasonal depression every year. With the passage of
time, these feelings of loss and loneliness intensified, and contributed significantly to Helen's inner questioning. In 1971, these
recurrent feelings also led to a melancholic period of self-doubt.
Helen soon began to mistrust her own sincerity of purpose, and,
unable to come to terms with her feelings, she poured out her mis-
givings and sorrow in a letter to Wilbur and Vera Davies:

I become more aware every day that I am just fooling myself when I say "I'M DOING THIS FOR GOD," for the best work you can do for GOD is done quietly and not always with the big PLUG, PUSH AND PROMOTION of yourself. It is true I get fabulous letters of praise and I tell myself I must answer them to help GOD, but it really is not helping HIM. It is just an effort to make myself a very desirable "little angel" in the eyes of my fans. We are all just playing GOD in some way or another. Now I must try to extricate myself from this. How I will do it, I do not know!!!???

By a twist of fate, the Davies stopped in Cincinnati on October 16, 1971, to visit with Helen just when she learned of Dorothy Gradison's untimely death. Given Helen's own feelings of vulnerability, the news that one of her closest friends had died came as a shock nearly beyond endurance. Helen knew that Dorothy Gradison was suffering from emphysema, but there was no warning that her condition was terminal. Indeed, Mrs. Gradison had visited Helen while at Gibson the day before her death to select Christmas cards, so Helen was all the more surprised; Dot had seemed so lively. To survive this unexpected crisis, Helen drew on her own belief that death was nothing more than a stepping-stone into eternal life, something she expressed in comforting Mrs. Gradison's elderly Aunt Edith:

> . . . and the sadness of her death is softened for me in knowing that she never had to linger in "THE TWILIGHT of LIFE" and become incapacitated and unable to be her own sweet, active, cheerful self. How wonderful to know that with one, swift, little step she crossed "THE THRESHOLD of ETERNITY. . . ."

To Willis Gradison, who had befriended her in the early 1930s and supported her throughout her career, Helen did everything she could to bring comfort. She wrote to Willis that he could count on her to help in any way she could, acknowledging that he must feel "utterly and completely inadequate to meet what looms ahead of you." She added that he had her prayers, and something that was probably more comforting, the sympathy of one who had experienced the same kind of loss:

> A "LIGHT" has gone out of your life, and now you must let your life become a prayer until you are strong enough to stand under the weight of your own thought again. But remember, "the same GOD who helped you before is ready and willing to help you once more!"

Prayer had always played an important role in Helen Steiner Rice's life. Now, in the aftermath of Dorothy Gradison's death, as Helen became more reflective, she found new comfort in the themes she had chosen for her fourth book, *Prayerfully*. Its publication in November 1971 gratified her more than anything else she had done, and prompted Helen to write enthusiastically to Mary Jane Ross: "Gee, <u>PRAYERFULLY</u> really seems to be just WHAT I DREAMED IT WOULD BE, for everybody seems to love it and its simplicity!"

A week later, when Helen went home to Lorain for Thanksgiving, she was astonished by the warm reception of one ardent follower. This particular fan, who worked as a remedial reading teacher, anticipated Helen's arrival at her favorite beauty parlor in Lorain. Driving there early, the lady waited patiently in blustery winter weather for Helen to arrive, and when she did, Helen found her admirer nearly buried in an armload of books. She held eight copies of *Prayerfully*, ten copies of *Lovingly*, three of *Heart Gifts*, and two of *Just for You*, all for Helen to autograph. Helen was immensely flattered. She later told her editor at Revell: "Of course, it was quite a job to do this autographing, (as my pinched nerve in my foot and my crumbling back were kicking up an awful rumpus), but I felt, since she was such a loyal fan and had hunted from Cleveland to Elyria to find these books, the least I could do was autograph them!" Helen was constantly astonished by the devotion of her admirers.

Revell's executives were elated by the success of Helen's work, so they naturally pressed her for another book. Eager to capitalize on Helen's popularity, the company urged her to finish it in time for a July 1972 publication date. It was no easy feat for a woman over seventy who was still going to Gibson each day to answer mail, but despite the pressure, she promised to do her best.

It proved to be a difficult promise for Helen to keep, for she found herself unexpectedly plunged into a period of great spiritual anguish. Always an extraordinarily sensitive person, as she matured Helen had become more attuned to the cycles of deepening faith within her. Ultimately, they enabled her first to understand, and then to describe quite clearly, the interior suffering brought on by what St. John of the Cross called "the dark night of the soul." Helen expressed the anguish she felt to those she believed would understand. One was Sister Louise, the nun who years before had brought a group of elderly visitors to Gibson. In a poignant letter, Helen told Sister Louise:

> I realize these periods do come, and the pain of them is much worse than physical pain. But I also realize these pains are so intense because I have been so blessed in always having such an AWARE-NESS of GOD'S PRESENCE. So, whenever these periods come and I feel there is a SHADOW hiding HIS FACE from me, it is like a GREAT BEREAVEMENT and my heart is broken. It has nothing to do with FAITH, for my FAITH remains the same. It is just that I want the joy of feeling HIM near to me. But I think HE sends these periods to make us realize that, even though we do not have this AWARENESS, HE is with us in the SHADOWS and loving us just as much as when we can feel HIS nearness. But it is an awful struggle trying to go through these times.

Helen's "dark hours of soul-searching" continued unabated for months. She found some relief, or at least distraction, in answering her mail at Gibson and completing her new book, *Someone Cares*, for Revell. Helen also wrote several new poems in an effort to impose order on her inner chaos. Even when her spirits reached rock bottom, she still managed to compose a humorous verse for Michael Neiheisel, an accountant with the firm of Arthur Young and Company, who prepared her April 1972 income tax form. It was vintage Helen, and something that her old friends, especially Willis Gradison, Sr., surely appreciated:

> *Taxes are something "I ungladly pay" . . .*
> *for there must be a more simple way . . .*
> *to figure out a tax return . . .*
> *on wages that you "slave to earn" . . . .*
> *But I guess if taxes were easy to do . . .*
> *there'd be no jobs for folks like you . . .*
> *and I am glad there is someplace to go . . .*
> *where there are competent people who know . . .*
> *how to decipher this Miserable Mess . . .*
> *and accurately (I hope) correctly assess . . .*
> *what I should pay at the end of the year . . .*
> *for the special privilege of living "here". . . .*
> *But believe it or not Mrs. Helen S. Rice . . .*
> *does not object "to the Government's price" . . .*
> *It's just that unfathomable 1040 form . . .*
> *that creates in me an "emotional storm."*

While she was consumed by her own spiritual crisis during the summer of 1972, Helen received a troubling letter from Mary Jane Ross. Like Phyllis Murphy before her, Mary Jane had come to believe that opportunities for women were limited at Revell, so she notified Helen that she was leaving the company. Helen was deeply saddened by the news, mostly because the relationship she had developed with Mary Jane Ross provided a touchstone for Helen's dealings with the publishing industry. The letter prompted Helen, not without some pain, to recall her own youth, when she was, as she put it, a "very zealous little suffragette." Although Helen claimed that time and experience had mellowed her, the spirit of that "outspoken fighter for women" was more vibrant in her aging body than she thought. Her response to Mary Jane would have struck a sympathetic chord in the Helen Steiner of 1925:

> And while I still fight hard for what I think is right, I do not make a major issue of it. . . . You see, Mary Jane, in my heart, nobody can downgrade me, and I just feel sorry for these pompous males who think they are outsmarting me. I don't let it disturb me to the point of demanding this. I just don't respect them as "my equals," although they think I am subservient to them. . . .
>
> . . . And, dear, if it makes men happy to feel superior to dominate women, that is fine. I'll just let them live in a "FOOL'S PARADISE," and I'll just go on and manage my life. And I have always gotten along very well with men.

When Helen returned home to Lorain for a visit with Gertrude in September, she hoped to be able to find solutions for some of the problems that confronted her. She was terribly disappointed, for her "night" of interior anguish only seemed to intensify. She confided to the Cuthbertsons, friends since her days with Ohio Public Service, that in her heart she understood the problem:

> But I know GOD is behind "THE DARK CLOUD" that engulfs me, and I must endure it until HE removes "THE DARKNESS," for this is not a DESTRUCTIVE EXPERIENCE but a CON-

STRUCTIVE ONE. I am sure HE is trying to awaken me to a NEW AWARENESS of how to best serve HIM, and after my old self dies completely, I know I will once again feel ebullient and lighthearted. But right now it is a struggle, and all I can do is just "HANG ON!" I have become so terribly tired, and it is an effort for me to do things that used to afford me so much pleasure. Yet somehow I keep doing things that are beyond all my limitations. But through it all, I keep realizing that I could never have done the things I have done on my OWN STRENGTH and POWER, and I know my SPIRITUAL RESOURCES have been given to me by GOD and people all over the world who pray for me.

Wracked as she was by spiritual turmoil and beset by physical ailments, Helen still managed to remember Willis Gradison during the celebration of Judaism's most sacred times, Rosh Hashanah and Yom Kippur. Thinking back to the 1930s, and the tribute he had written to her so long ago, Helen wrote to Willis: "I still think that these HIGH HOLY DAYS are like no other holidays and that everybody in the world should set aside a time to reflect on their conduct during the year and to join in a spirit of penitence and reverence."

Ironically, the same Helen who gathered accolades from others for working miracles in their lives spent much of her time rooting out personal imperfections she saw in herself; to Helen, they were flaws that barred her path to God. In a letter to Mary Jane Ross, she tried to answer the thorny question of "just how far GOD really wants me to go":

There are times when I think it is even arrogant of me to have found so much pride and pleasure in my writings, and I know how happy I was when <u>SOMEONE CARES</u> was published in such a beautiful way. But our society in this world seems to make different people out of us, and we all "masquerade," and sometimes it is difficult to find out just who we are ourselves.

Helen
Steiner Rice
Ambassador
of Sunshine

My problem is not dying. It is LIVING! I am so completely consumed with the desire to live each day of my life ABUNDANTLY in the service of THE LORD that to be limited and confined to living it at a slower pace and curtailing all my activities "saddens my soul."

Helen found solace in realizing she was undergoing the same inner trials that men and women of deep faith had always experienced. Her constant comfort was the Bible, something she freely admitted to her friend Jean Bolton:

Each day I become more aware that all these things I am experiencing have been felt by others on down through the centuries, and never has it been so vivid to me as when I read PSALM 102. I can hear myself saying these same words, asking GOD to "hear my prayer and not to hide HIS FACE," and I, too, feel that "my days vanish like smoke" and "my heart is stricken." So, in reading through passages in THE BIBLE, I realize this is GOD and that HE is trying once more to TAKE ME and BREAK ME and MAKE ME JUST WHAT HE WANTS ME TO BE!

Just as Helen felt battered by God on the inside, she was also being shaped by pressures in her daily life. Her latest book, *Someone Cares*, was selling so well that Bill Barbour, the president of Revell, began pressing her to write another one. Meanwhile, Pyramid, a company specializing in paperbacks, published one of Helen's collections entitled *Everyone Needs Someone*. Then, like an unwelcome cold shower, Helen received a notice from the Internal Revenue Service that they had decided to audit her tax returns.

Evidently what worried the I.R.S. most was that Helen claimed to have contributed so much to churches. For the first time in all her years of selfless giving to religious institutions, Helen found herself in the odd position of having to verify every one of her donations. "If you have never been audited by the I.R.S., I shall pray that you never will be!" Helen cautioned Audrey Carroll. Once her anger had subsided and Helen analyzed the problem, she realized the root of her problem: "so few people seem to believe in tithing and fewer still in overtithing." More bemused than irritated by the experience, Helen finally resolved the issue by writing to the I.R.S.: "All you can do is penalize me in the only way you know, for I am going to 'WORRY NO MORE FOR GOD KNOWS THE SCORE' and 'IF GOD BE FOR YOU, WHO CAN BE AGAINST YOU' . . . except the I.R.S.!" The government's hard-eyed bureaucrats probably didn't understand her humor, but at least she escaped their scrutiny for the moment.

The government did not, however, escape Helen's scrutiny. She was revolted by the growing Watergate scandal, and confided to Audrey Carroll, "It disturbs my whole inner being to realize that a situation like WATERGATE is not only a POLITICAL PROBLEM but a PERSONAL PART of our EVERYDAY LIVING, for our entire society is structured on manipulation, intrigue, conspiracy, complicity, and misrepresentation." Yet even though chaos seemed to engulf the world around her, by late summer 1973, Helen was able to report to Audrey that something very important had transpired in her spiritual life. Her dark night of the soul had lifted:

> I will not attempt to tell you all the things that have happened to me this summer and are still happening. But through it all what I once believed was a satisfying relationship with GOD has "opened up like a flower in the sun," and I find . . . that I really never knew "THE WONDER OF HIM," for I think I could not live long enough to comprehend it all!

Helen understood that even though things were much better spiritually, her new awareness had not solved all her everyday problems. It merely armed her to meet the challenges she would have to face in the final years of her life. The aging process, she wrote to Dora Fischer in February 1974, was like slowly going up in an airplane: "The HORIZON gets WIDER and WIDER as we look down on this earth, and things become SMALLER and SMALLER and of MUCH LESS IMPORTANCE in the PANORAMIC VIEW of OUR SOUL!" That new vision, she explained, made her realize that "all this world has to give me is fleeting." It was a wise and spiritually mature Helen Steiner Rice who revealed to her friend, "I find my GREATEST SOURCE of COMFORT and the ONLY THING that can lift me above my 'EARTHLY BONDAGE' is to be ALONE with GOD."

259

Like a
Flower
in the
Sun

9

*Please
Make
My Next
Move
to Heaven*

*a*s Helen Steiner Rice grew older, she slowly came to understand the inevitability of change. It was a hard lesson, but she learned it well. One of the most difficult adjustments she had to make to the forces of change came in the twilight of her life, when Helen, then nearly 75 years of age, found it necessary to look for a new home.

More than forty years had passed since Helen had moved into her room at the Gibson Hotel on Fifth Street in downtown Cincinnati. She had spent more time in that small—and often lonely—room than anywhere else during her entire life, so Helen understandably thought of it as home. Consequently, her ties to her modest quarters at the Gibson Hotel proved stronger, despite her fondest childhood memories, than her affection for the house on Reid Avenue in Lorain. Because of those deeply rooted feelings, she was shaken to the core when she learned, early in 1974, that the Gibson would soon be torn down. After all, the hotel had become, at least in her mind, a refuge from life's tribulations; it was really more than home. At first, she was speechless at the prospect of seeing her home destroyed, but she eventually regained her composure and was able to express her dismay. Writing to Audrey Carroll, Helen described the announcement as a

Helen's friend, Jack Wiedemer, helped her relocate to the Cincinnati Club when the Gibson Hotel closed in 1974.

"bombshell" that shattered her completely. "MOVING BECOMES A REAL MENACE!" she exclaimed, for someone who has accumulated forty years of "mess and mass."

Helen's reaction to the razing of the Gibson Hotel had two distinct facets. Psychologically, she simply could not come to grips with the notion that her refuge—carefully decorated over the years with everyday items that provided an indispensable lifeline—was to be leveled by a wrecking crew. Practically, Helen found herself in a dither over the news, for she had no idea where she would go once she was evicted. Worse yet, she was frightened by the prospect of relocating. She had relied so long on the Gibson Hotel and its staff that she felt incapable of adjusting to such a far-reaching

Please
Make
My
Next
Move
to Heaven

change in her daily routine. "Would you believe," she told Gibson coworker Bob Reis, "a woman my age can't make a bed or do cleaning? I really don't remember how. It's been too long since I've been without daily maid service!" In more philosophical letters to her friends, Helen put the whole matter into God's hands: "I do know for sure that GOD will manage it in HIS WAY. And since we both know that HIS WAY is always the right way, I will accept it as another GIFT of HIS LOVE."

Fortunately for Helen "God's will" was made known through the practical wisdom of her old friend, Jack Wiedemer. When Mr. Wiedemer learned that the Gibson Hotel was about to be torn down, he was immediately concerned about where Helen would go. When he encountered her at work one day, Jack asked what arrangements she had made. Just as distraught then as she was when she first heard that the Gibson would be demolished, Helen simply told him that she was waiting for God to lead the way. As sensitive as he was perceptive, Jack Wiedemer asked, "Helen, would you mind if I gave God a lift on this thing?" Once again, Helen's basic decency and caring attitude toward her peers was reciprocated. With careful attention to Helen's needs and feelings, Jack Wiedemer made arrangements for her to move into a suite at the Cincinnati Club, a residential hotel not far from the Gibson. To someone in Helen's vulnerable position, what Mr. Wiedemer did was an extraordinary act of kindness that could never be sufficiently rewarded.

Once steps had been taken to arrange new living conditions for Helen, she began to stew about the details of moving. While her worries eventually proved groundless, they nevertheless aroused terrible fears that she would be evicted from the Gibson Hotel before her quarters at the Cincinnati Club were ready. "Each night I just go home and look at that cluttered up room and wonder if it is going to be possible for me to go through this," she wrote to Audrey Carroll toward the end of May 1974. "If I could just

Helen
Steiner Rice
*Ambassador
of Sunshine*

somehow close the door and walk out of that room without one thing, IT WOULD BE THE BEST THING THAT COULD HAPPEN TO ME. But, if we are going to continue to live, we do have to perform like normal human beings, and somehow this must all be taken care of!"

Helen always tried to find the spiritual dimension to life's challenges, and the move to the Cincinnati Club gave her an opportunity to apply her philosophy in a way she never could have anticipated. Clearly agitated by the way her life had been disturbed, she wrote: "Of course, having to look for NEW SURROUNDINGS at this stage of life has added to INTENSIFY my LONGING to MOVE to MY ETERNAL HOME, which will be completely furnished and I will not have to go through the trauma of packing a FORTY-YEAR ACCUMULATION of FURNITURE and FURBELOWS." Just as he had earlier, Jack Wiedemer sensed the pain her move from the Gibson caused Helen, so he once again "gave God a hand" by hiring a driver with a station wagon to move Helen and her belongings over the few blocks—to Helen it must have seemed like a continent—from the dying Gibson Hotel to a new life and new rooms in the Cincinnati Club.

Aside from the inconvenience, Helen's relocation from the Gibson was psychologically exhausting and physically depleting. Earlier that year, more spinal discs had disintegrated, and she developed a heart condition after her rib cage slipped over the right lung, cutting off most of its oxygen supply. Depressed, short of breath, and limited in mobility, she lost thirty pounds during the move. She felt that most of her energy had been dissipated in an effort that was hardly worth the trouble. By the end of July, however, Helen had settled into her new quarters at the Cincinnati Club, and the terrors of abandoning the doomed Gibson Hotel were fading faster than she had ever expected. Once she had acclimated herself to the new surroundings, Helen even found she was able to complete another book for Revell, tentatively entitled *Life*

Is Forever. Ever striving to adjust and to remain optimistic, she reported to Johnnie and Ruby Sullivan, friends she often dined with at Wong's Chinese Restaurant:

> I just want to tell you that I am gradually becoming organized again! While things are still in a STATE of LIMBO, I have moved into THE CINCINNATI CLUB, and I am sure in time I will come to like it very much. However, MOVING, after 40 years of being at THE GIBSON HOTEL and at my age, certainly was a TRAUMATIC EXPERIENCE and I really never want to go through it again! Daily I say when I pray . . . 'DEAR GOD, please make my next move to HEAVEN,' for I can just soar peacefully on 'THE WINGS of FAITH' into THE PROMISED LAND where my NEW ETERNAL HOME awaits me in MY MANSION IN THE SKY!

The affirmation of friends helped Helen cut all ties to the now-defunct Gibson Hotel, and the letters she received from around the world motivated her to continue her ministry. Once the move was behind her, Helen had the opportunity to go through her mail. She told Ernie Bein, pastor of the relocated Wesley Chapel, how astonished she was by the "staggering accumulation of letters from people seeking a haven for their troubled hearts and trying to find an answer that only GOD can give." Reverend Bein was certain that Helen Steiner Rice suffered when she opened every envelope. Once he found Helen crying in her office over a message she had received. It was from a woman asking for advice on how to deal with the aftermath of her husband's suffocation in a snowdrift. Letters such as these, Helen explained, made her ever more aware that she could not "falter now just because the load is becoming more than my decreasing physical capacities can seemingly carry." She confided to Reverend Bein that the one thing she wanted to do most of all in the world was to keep answering her mail as long as possible.

Helen
Steiner Rice
Ambassador
of Sunshine

Despite her deepening spirituality, Helen found herself progressively less able to attend Sunday services. Painfully conscious of her absence from church, she explained to her pastor that it was due to the fact that she pushed herself beyond endurance during the week, then found great peace on weekends in quiet meditation alone in her room. Vexed beyond measure by her physical limitations, she wrote:

> It seems right now I want to go DIRECTLY to GOD, for I want to know HIM BETTER AND TO BECOME ONE WITH HIM . . . and to do this means that I must LOSE MYSELF IN SILENCE. That is why I am not quite ready to come back to WESLEY . . . but you do know I am there in SPIRIT every Sunday.

That was one thing Ernie Bein had no question about, for Helen's presence in his congregation had long been an inspiration to him. He vividly recalled how she would put her head back and close her eyes during his sermon. Some members of the congregation would smirk, laugh silently, and wink at one another, thinking that she had fallen asleep, but they were wrong. In fact, she was focusing her concentration on what was being said, something Reverend Bein understood fully, for when he spoke to Helen as she was leaving church, she would invariably summarize his lesson for the day. "She wasn't asleep," he reported many years later; "she blanked everything else out so she could listen very intently to the sermon. It was such a joy because I knew nobody else in that room heard anything I was saying. She heard everything."

Limiting though her physical ailments were, Helen made the most of her waning energy. She tried to view her handicaps as opportunities to explore her relationship with God. Since she was no longer able to go out for dinner in the evening as she had in the past, she frequently wrapped up food from Gibson's cafeteria, where she usually ate lunch, and took it home to warm as her

Helen grew more reflective as her life neared its end, but she tried hard to answer the many letters from those who loved her verses and sought advice.

Helen
Steiner Rice
*Ambassador
of Sunshine*

evening meal. Afterward, in the quiet of her room, exhausted by her day at work and her constant difficulty in breathing, she turned to rest and meditation. "I may feel a little lonely at times," she wrote to a friend in Dayton, "but I am NEVER ALONE. I know my loneliness is just the SOUL trying to get back to the place it came from, and GOD IS NEVER MORE THAN A PRAYER AWAY."

Like many people in their final years, Helen spent much of her free time reflecting on the blessings of the present while she pondered experiences of the past. Among her greatest blessings, Helen included her relationship with Mary Jo Eling. "It is almost unbelievable that one so young and filled with life and vivacity could be so sensitive and introspective," she exclaimed to Audrey Carroll. When Miss Eling was called to jury duty in 1975, Helen wrote in support of her request to be excused, citing the significance of Mary Jo's role in helping Helen respond to the spiritual needs of thousands:

> We are engaged in a very important and worldwide Inspirational ministry, and it took me eight years to familiarize her with this work, so that she has become an integral part of the ministry. . . . To be robbed of her services for even a few weeks would be a great loss to everyone who so needs this kind of help in these uncertain days of violence and confusion.

Another personification of blessing was Bill Stewart, a gentleman she met when Gibson stopped running its commuter bus to the Amberley Village plant. A messenger and driver for Gibson, Mr. Stewart's principal duty was shuttling from Amberley Village to downtown Cincinnati to pick up Gibson's mail. When the commuter service was discontinued, Helen worried about how she would get to work, but she could have saved herself the strain. Jack Wiedemer once again came to her rescue by arranging for Stewart to call for Helen each morning when he drove into the city and drop her off at the Cincinnati Club in the afternoon. It was a perfect arrangement for everyone concerned, and the more Helen came to know Bill Stewart, the more she believed that God had sent him to support and uplift her. "Bill is an unbelievably good driver and such a gentleman," she reported to Audrey Carroll. But he was a great deal more. Like Mary Jo Eling, Bill Stewart reassured Helen that she was not alone.

The affirmation of Helen Steiner Rice's blessings was offset somewhat by recollections of the past. Inevitably, when Helen reminisced, her mind drifted to memories of Franklin. In August 1975, just weeks after the publication of *Loving Promises*, Helen disclosed to her friend, Evelyn Dratt, that she believed everything in her life had been sent to teach her lessons for living. Franklin's death, she revealed, was the most important instruction of all:

> I have been rereading some of the old letters that Franklin had written to me during those desperate days of the Great Depression, and they awakened many memories. All that was beyond my understanding then, now I see as part of GOD'S PLAN. I know Franklin's "GOING OUT" was my "COMING IN," for I never could have written these poems or had the compassion for others that I now have if he had not decided to go to meet death before death came to meet him.

Helen echoed the same sentiment to Reverend Bein, explaining that Franklin's death had refocused her life and given her a perspective she could never have found otherwise. "Before Franklin died," she told him, "I was a piece of fluff—there was nothing to my life—it was all fun, and I mean I was counting for nothing. The death of Franklin is what God used to make me a person of substance, and to do things for His benefit and not my own."

The nature and extent of Helen's spiritual thought was never expressed more clearly than in September 1975, when she was contacted by a man writing a book on life after death. He asked her to respond to the question: "Assuming there is a life after death, and that when one arrives on the other side one can meet whomever he chooses, what person would you most like to meet . . . and what would you like to talk about with this other person?"

Helen began her response aggressively, writing: "In the first place, I am not ASSUMING that THERE IS LIFE AFTER DEATH. I KNOW THERE IS!" Having left no doubt about where she stood, she continued:

> I was not familiar with the earth before I arrived here. The CREATOR got me safely here, and so HE will take me safely back with-

out me knowing the full particulars. If we could answer all these questions about LIFE AFTER DEATH that are tossed about with reckless abandon, we certainly would have no need for FAITH and EVERYTHING WOULD LOSE ITS ENTIRE MEANING and PURPOSE. The ways of the CREATOR are unfathomable, and I am too busy trying to "walk in HIS FOOTSTEPS" and making the most of "my sojourn on earth" to spend any time on what ETERNITY holds for me.

Our "GRADUATION to GLORY" is a SPIRITUAL THING. I do not think it will be confined to any little, mundane limitation, and I am quite sure nobody will gravitate instantly into the arms of one, certain individual, for that would be making ETERNITY a little too EARTHLY.

Helen concluded her response by promising to mail the researcher a copy of her book *Life Is Forever*. She also tried to broaden his horizons, writing: "I think it will give you a good idea of how limited the thinking is of those who, for one reason or another, want to meet some special person and start this earthly existence all over again." For Helen Steiner Rice, whose life had been transformed by the loss of one special person, the truth of these words was the result of experience.

Her mind clearly intact and active, Helen seemed to all the world as vibrant as she had been for decades, but in truth, her physical decline continued at a frightening pace. Along with everything else, new heart problems emerged to complicate her spinal difficulties. "I am deteriorating daily," she told Audrey. "But somehow with each experience the 'AMAZING GRACE of GOD' looms ever more unfathomable and more wonderful." In April 1976, some of the discs in her back deteriorated further without warning when she was entering her room at the Cincinnati Club; Helen tried to put the happiest face on the crisis. Ever optimistic, she chose to view her prolonged hospital stay as a gift from God. Despite her pain, she wrote to a friend, Jerry Gifford:

Please

Make

My

Next

Move

to Heaven

Since April 30, my life has been "touched by GOD," and everything has been completely changed, both physically and spiritually. And while this unexpected encounter with pain (which rendered me completely helpless) may be distressing at times, in GOD'S HANDS it is really a BLESSING. I have always been very impatient about everything, and this is making me aware that, if I want to be a true disciple of THE LORD, I must "take up my cross and follow HIM," for no one belongs on "GOD'S ROAD" if he has "no cross to carry."

Once Helen's condition had stabilized and the physicians had prescribed treatment, she discovered exactly how much of a "cross" she would have to bear. A significant part of it was wearing a heavy and cumbersome back brace. Just strapping the device on drained the energy and tried the patience of a woman whose entire life had rested on her hardiness and independence. By the end of June, Helen was so frustrated that she lamented to Jerry Gifford:

I wish I could write to you and tell you that I am "SITTING ON TOP OF THE WORLD," filled with renewed enthusiasm and endless zip, zest, zeal, and zing. But trying to wear this back brace presents unbelievable problems. No matter how valiantly I try, I just cannot seem to get into this heavy horrendous contraption by myself. I am willing and eager to try to wear it regardless of the undesirableness of walking around in a strait jacket looking like the "HUNCHBACK OF NOTRE DAME." But I am certainly accepting this as one of THE GREATEST GIFTS GOD ever sent to me, for I realize now that only HIS LOVE and WISDOM could have known that I needed this brace not only for MY BACK but for MY SOUL.

Things were so difficult for Helen that she asked her sister, Gertrude, to come to Cincinnati to keep her company and lend moral support. Gertrude spent a month with Helen, helping her in and out of the back brace and encouraging her sister in a desperate struggle with the ravages of old age. To her credit, Helen refused to let her trials and tribulations get her down. Instead, she used Gertrude's help and advice to reassert her own independence. On June 25, 1975, she wrote to Audrey Carroll: "Soon I must start trying to make it on my own, for the longer I postpone this, the weaker and more unsteady I become. So I think when she [Gertrude] leaves next week, I'm going to try to go to my office for a short time each day . . . and I'm sure with GOD'S HELP this will be possible." Her determination was eventually rewarded with the ability to master the brace, which made possible an occasional return to her office at Gibson. For someone in Helen's physical condition, her resolve was a courageous demonstration of mind over matter.

At the time of her hospitalization, Helen was immersed in work on yet another volume of poems to be published by Revell. She had no idea how she would ever produce a new book in the face of such pain and distraction, but her spirit was so great that *Somebody Loves You* was actually finished while she was in the hospital. The quality of the work was a testament to the virtues of adversity, for Revell's president, Bill Barbour, expressed the greatest delight with the manuscript. His response cheered Helen who, as always, saw God's plan in her success. "The Lord stepped in and helped me to complete it," she later told her old friends, Frances and Ross Page, "and every word in that entire book, I borrowed from HIM, and it has turned out to be the best book I have ever written, according to the publishers."

When the first copy reached her on October 11, 1976, Helen stayed up until 2 A.M. reading every line with care. When she had finished, Helen wrote to Ann Curtiss at Revell: "I am ECSTATI-CALLY ENTHUSED and SPIRITUALLY SATISFIED. . . . Receiving and reading SOMEBODY LOVES YOU was 'SPIRI-TUAL SUNSHINE' for my sometimes discouraging days. . . ."

Over the following months, Helen strove to adjust to a new lifestyle imposed by her physical handicaps. She had hoped that by

Easter 1977, more than a year after her hospitalization, she might be able to visit her office more regularly to handle correspondence. She quickly learned that anything more than intermittent, short periods of work was beyond her tolerance. It was hard for Helen to accept, but by the spring of 1977, when she found herself still acknowledging Christmas remembrances, she wrote a belated thank-you note to Hallie Herbstreit, explaining her tardiness with humor and regret:

> . . . things keep happening all the time, and for some unknown reason, GOD certainly is trying to find out if I really have what it takes to "TRAVEL ON THE HEAVENLY HIGHWAY." Right now I am stumbling over a new roadblock. . . . It seems that in addition to all my other little physical "obstacles," the sciatic nerve in my right side has joined "the wrecking crew." It's almost laughable to see them tearing THE OLD GIBSON HOTEL down and to know that I am going right along with it!

Anyone who knew Helen Steiner Rice would expect her to laugh outwardly at her own decline, but at the same time her introspective nature demanded that she search for the meaning of her suffering. At the end of July, she tried to express her desire to live up to what God expected in a letter to Ruby and Johnnie Sullivan:

> When this physical cross was first given to me, my acceptance seemed so joyous in the first few months of my "journey" on "THE KING'S HIGHWAY." But as new physical limitations keep being added one by one, I keep wishing that GOD would give me HIS LOVING REASSURANCE that HE is not disappointed because now and then I do falter under the WEIGHT of the CROSS, which I realize HE has given to me as a GIFT and not as a HINDRANCE.

With Ernie Bein's help, Helen eventually discovered a new perspective from which to examine her own suffering. Together, they reflected on a prayer she had written in 1973, which began with the lines: "Take me and break me and make me, dear GOD, Just what you want me to be. . . ." It was, in fact, Helen's favorite among her many verses; it had been written at a time when her incredible successes seemed to indicate God's goodness all around her. She took the opportunity to let her pastor know that God had indeed answered her bold prayer and was now trusting Helen to keep her word. Helen found new joy in that awareness, and expressed it to Reverend Bein in a letter:

> When pain became pleasure, I knew at last without any doubt that GOD had approved of my every spoken word and I knew beyond words to express that GOD is more than I ever dared to trust my inner feelings to convey to me. So, all I can say is . . . GOD, YOU do hear every prayer and you do answer every prayer, and I am waiting for YOU to take me HOME.

Eager though she was for "her heavenly home," Helen realized that there were earthly matters that also needed attention. She had, for instance, carefully followed the lives of the Gradison children. Young Bill Gradison's political career, first as city councilman and then as congressman, reminded Helen so much of his father's public service that she eagerly supported his endeavors. She was no less interested in the life of Joan Gradison Coe.

In 1977, Joan was summoned from Massachusetts by her father to attend a special meeting with Helen in Cincinnati. Willis Gradison, Sr., gave Joan instructions to have a new, floor-length gown made for the occasion. Joan and her father appeared on a designated evening at Helen's suite in the Cincinnati Club. Decked out in bright colors, with her hair piled high, Helen met them at the elevator, and ushered two of her favorite people into her apartment for a formal presentation. There, Helen bestowed on her "Joanie" a substantial block of Cincinnati Milacron stock, which she had transferred to Joan's name! Helen also wrote Joan a special poem for the occasion, recalling a relationship that had endured for decades:

THIS IS MORE THAN JUST A PRESENT...
IT'S A GIFT OF LOVE, MY DEAR...
AND IT'S PROMPTED BY FOND
*   MEMORIES...*
THAT GROW DEARER YEAR BY YEAR...
FOR MEMORIES ARE A TREASURE...
BORN OF YESTERDAY'S BRIGHT JOY...
THAT BUILD LITTLE PATHWAYS THROUGH
*   OUR HEARTS...*
THAT TIME CANNOT DESTROY...
AND WHILE OUR "PATHS" WENT
*   DIFFERENT WAYS...*
I STILL REMEMBER THOSE "LONG-AGO
*   DAYS"...*
AND THIS "TOKEN" IS GIVEN IN FOND
*   RECOLLECTION...*
OF FORTY-FOUR YEARS OF SPECIAL
*   AFFECTION!*

For nearly as long as she could remember, Helen had relied on Willis Gradison's guidance in money matters, and his advice had helped her amass a modest fortune. When Mr. Gradison died in August 1978, little more than a month after suffering a serious fall, Helen lost both a sage adviser and one of her dearest friends. This terrible blow came at a time in Helen's life when her resiliency was at low ebb, and the tragedy was intensified because she could not travel to the hospital to see her old friend before he passed away. In her grief, Helen wrote to Mary Barbour on September 14: "There is so much that has happened in these several months that

I don't think I will ever be able to in any way explain the anguish I have gone through, and I don't mean physical pain, because I have learned to live with that."

Helen felt Willis Gradison's loss in ways too numerous to mention. For decades, he had been her confidant, a sounding board for ideas, a trustworthy refuge from the world of corporate politics, and a savvy financial consultant. Without his counsel, Helen was very much at sea, particularly in financial matters. Unaccustomed to dealing personally with such issues, she felt overwhelmed by the most basic fiscal requirements—the need to file estimated taxes and calculate deductions. In a moment of despair, she cried out to Mary Barbour, "I am so sick and tired of seeing estimates and figures, if I never see one again in my life, I'll be HAPPY!"

For years, Helen had resisted the clamor of her fans for a detailed account of her life, preferring to let her writings "speak" for her. By 1978, however, she reconsidered, acceding to suggestions that thousands could benefit from an understanding of the trail that had led her to so many good works. Consequently, she agreed, in 1978, to give a series of interviews about her memories and philosophy to *Guideposts* editor Fred Bauer. The result was a memoir, *In the Vineyard of the Lord,* published by Revell in 1979.

Helen continued to adjust her outlook and contend with constantly changing pressures as she reconciled herself to failing health. On December 1, 1978, she wrote to Kathleen Mimms about how difficult it was to face the realization that she was becoming a burden to others. Yet Helen's indomitable spirit kept her from being overcome by depression and indulging in self-pity. In spite of the somber topic, Helen included a dose of self-mockery and humor in her response to one of Miss Mimms's letters by referring to an earlier observation about the aging process:

I remember so well writing a poem some years ago saying . . .
"GROWING OLDER ONLY MEANS THAT OUR LIVES ARE

MORE SERENE." But sometimes I say to myself . . . "AM I REALLY HANDLING MY LIMITATIONS WITH GRACE?" You know when I first went to the hospital several years ago, I told myself, "THIS, TOO, WILL PASS AWAY." But that, evidently was not GOD'S PLAN for my life, and my physical limitations have kept multiplying until we no longer seem to have enough space to list them all on the Medicare Report. . . .

Her reflectiveness was typical of the tactics Helen Steiner Rice employed in surviving from day to day, tactics that were, above everything else, grounded in practicality. At age seventy-nine, with deteriorating health, she was well aware of her responsibility to make some painful but necessary decisions about what would become of her estate after her death. By 1979, Helen Steiner Rice was receiving royalties from her books in excess of $100,000 a year, and she had long ago decided that her assets should be used for the best possible purpose when she was gone. Again, Helen confided her innermost thoughts on the subject to Mary Barbour: "If I knew a way to give everything away and just erase this 'whole nightmare from my mind,' I think I'd be satisfied to just walk and talk with JESUS on my own and let the rest of the world go by!" But she knew that her desire, admirable though it was, would not be practical in a world of tax returns, balance sheets, investment credits, and dozens of other considerations, so she began to concentrate on the idea of using her accumulated wealth for charitable purposes.

The desire to give everything away soon became central to Helen's thoughts of the future, and it grew stronger as time passed. Her feelings were certainly nothing new, for over the years she had contributed huge sums of money to a variety of projects, especially ones sponsored by churches in Lorain and Cincinnati. She had also supported the work of The Salvation Army, the Little Sisters of the Poor, and numerous other charities, while giving thousands of dollars to individuals in need, frequently noting in the margins of letters she received: "sent check for $1000.00." At the bottom of Helen's generosity was a belief, based on Christ's teachings, that it is important to keep one's life "free of the love of money." Indeed, in her later years, she often wrote to her friends that she had always been guided by that philosophy. The more she thought about the various issues involved, the more she felt drawn to those who had been less fortunate than herself. In the end, she resolved to use her resources to serve the needy after she died.

Once she had arrived at her decision, the only thing that remained was determining how to convert her wishes into reality. In the past, Helen would have turned to Willis Gradison for help; she now looked to his son for advice. By this time, Bill Gradison was a rising young congressman, deeply involved in federal government, and much as he cared for "Aunt Helen," he felt her interests would be better served if she let a local expert on trusts and estates advise her. Accordingly, Willis introduced her to long-time friend and colleague, Cincinnati attorney Eugene Ruehlmann, who specialized in estate planning.

At their first meeting, which took place in Helen's office at Gibson, she did all the talking. Helen had formed specific plans about the disposition of her worldly goods, so her main concern was to make sure that Mr. Ruehlmann clearly understood her wishes. Her first desire was to ensure that her sister, Gertrude, would always be well cared for; secondly, Helen wanted assurances that her assets would be used to help the poor, the sick, and the needy. Once he understood her aims, Mr. Ruehlmann advised Helen to set up a charitable foundation to be funded by the assets of her estate after her death. The two hit it off from the beginning, for Ruehlmann's expertise meshed perfectly with Helen's aspirations, so in far less time than she had expected, the Helen Steiner Rice Foundation was incorporated.

Her farsighted financial planning collided, however, with one of the saddest memories of Helen's life. October 1979 marked the fiftieth anniversary of the Great Crash of 1929, an event seared in Helen's memory because it was so closely linked to the ruin and subsequent death of Franklin Rice. Knowing that October memories were the most agonizing ones for Helen and realizing that the newspapers were filled with retrospective accounts of the 1929 crash, Ernie Bein took time out to write an encouraging letter to Helen. The fact that he remembered her feelings about the anniversary touched Helen deeply. It opened a floodgate of emotion that allowed her to vent feelings she had kept in check for decades:

> October never engulfed me more deeply with "heart-hurt" than this October. . . . This year it seemed that the entire month of October was woven of nothing but teardrops and heartaches, and somehow the remembrance of Franklin's tragic departure into the UNKNOWN seemed to engulf me in loneliness and longing. . . . Of course, I realize that, as my own life ebbs away, I no longer can suppress my yearning for "GOD'S TOMORROW."

Shortly afterward, early in 1980, Helen spoke openly in a profile published in *Christian Life* magazine, of longing to move on to her "heavenly home." Helen told the reporter that an admirer had once suggested that when she died, the world would be deprived of the words she might yet write. Helen responded that she had already put into writing the lessons God had taught her, and felt she could go to her grave certain that God would find another to take up the work. Her modesty was admirable in view of the fact that, by 1980, sales of her cards had topped seventy-five million while purchases of her books passed the two-million mark. The distribution of innumerable calendars, plaques, stationery packages, booklets, records, and cassette tapes, all carrying Helen's words to people around the world, only offered more convincing evidence of Helen's stature in the international community.

As she approached her ninth decade, Helen assured Ernie Bein that she was still "struggling to work 'IN THE VINEYARD OF

THE LORD,'" even while she looked ahead to "GOD'S TOMORROW." For Helen, that meant continuing to go to her office at Gibson Greetings to answer mail whenever she was able. On April 21, 1980, as she was struggling out of the Gibson car at the front of the company's building in Amberley Village, she fell, breaking both her left hip and wrist. The injuries left her completely incapacitated.

Lying helpless in her hospital bed, Helen had plenty of time to consider the circumstances that left her anticipating her eightieth birthday under such depressing conditions. A flood of greetings from around the world acknowledging her birthday cheered and encouraged her just as she was preparing herself for one more move. When she had healed as much as her body was able, she was transferred from a local hospital to the Franciscan Terrace nursing home in Wyoming, a northern suburb of Cincinnati. Heartfelt messages from Pope John Paul II and President and Mrs. Jimmy Carter made the ordeal more tolerable. Additionally, the City of Cincinnati helped celebrate her eightieth birthday by proclaiming May 19, 1980, Helen Steiner Rice Day, which gave the staff at Franciscan Terrace a good reason to stage a party in her honor.

From her fifth-floor room at Franciscan Terrace, Helen could look down into a courtyard filled with blooming flowers while she recovered from her injuries. Having spent most of her life at the Gibson Hotel in downtown Cincinnati, it was the first such view Helen ever had, and she told Bob Reis, one of her daily visitors, that she thought it was the most beautiful place in Cincinnati. But even while she appreciated her new surroundings and came to love them, Helen occasionally found herself plagued by doubts. She expressed them occasionally to Mr. Reis, one day asking him, "Bob, do you think God will think I'm a fake?" Understanding that self-doubt was a normal part of every sensitive person's makeup, he did his best to calm Helen's fears.

Even in her final months, when it became clear to everyone who knew Helen that her life was ebbing away, she still had the clarity of vision to teach important lessons to her visitors. When Eugene Ruehlmann visited, for example, hoping to cheer Helen up, he usually came away feeling the tables had been turned. Instead of making Helen feel better, he found his own spirits lifted, "because she just radiated happiness and good cheer."

Her old friend Jack Wiedemer found her rather irritable on one visit, and wondered if she really wanted him to come back. Later, he was reminded of the importance of not neglecting the people who have given joy to our lives, so he returned. It was a wise decision, for this time Helen was her usual, jovial self, jokingly introducing him to a nurse as the former Gibson vice president who had always been "two steps ahead of the sheriff." Mr. Wiedemer was gratified by the quip for it reminded him of all the friendly, brisk exchanges that had enriched their relationship over the years.

On Saturday, March 14, 1981, in a private ceremony at Franciscan Terrace, Helen Steiner Rice was awarded an honorary Doctor of Humane Letters degree from the College of Mount St. Joseph. Helen, who once sacrificed the dream of a college education to help care for her family, was overwhelmed by the distinction. It was a fitting capstone to an exceptional life, and Sister Jean Patrice Harrington, S.C., president of the college, neatly summarized Helen's contributions when she acknowledged her visionary belief in the "right and ability of women to win their way in the world," and gave her long-due credit as a woman "dedicated to high ideals and a humane concern for others."

Helen Steiner Rice died a month after receiving her degree, on Thursday evening, April 23, 1981. The memorial card at her funeral featured Albrecht Dürer's "Praying Hands." After the service, Helen's remains were transported back to Lorain, where she was buried in Elmwood Cemetery, next to her parents.

Shortly before her death in 1981, Helen set up the Helen Steiner Rice Foundation to benefit the poor and elderly.

Even in death, Helen Steiner Rice did her best to ensure that her personal ministry to those in need would continue. The Helen Steiner Rice Foundation, funded by Helen's estate, was given the charge of distributing income from her endowment. Additionally,

Please Make My Next Move to Heaven

she bequeathed to the Foundation all of her personal correspondence, writings, artistic compositions, and other materials that might be used to generate further income. In the years after Helen's death, the Foundation, administered by Virginia J. Ruehlmann, has published fifteen books based on her works. The royalties from those publications, combined with the interest earned through the wise investment management of Helen's original bequest by the Gradison Company, made it possible, since 1982, for the Helen Steiner Rice Foundation to grant nearly 1.5 million dollars to charitable agencies.

It is impossible to assess the impact of Helen Steiner Rice's life. Throughout her career, Helen's verses brought comfort and inspiration to more people than can be counted, but unlike many others whose popularity fell as quickly as it rose, she continues to spread her message. She has been dead for many years, but people still want to hear what she had to say. Perhaps it is all part of what Helen viewed as adding human links to a "chain of love" around the world. It may also be something beyond human understanding. Frances Helms, one of Helen's most faithful correspondents, once wrote that Helen met the need within each human soul to be led simply, lovingly, and gently into God's presence. Helen's pastor, Ernie Bein, said simply, there were no words "to fully show in detail who and whose she was."